Mometrix
TEST PREPARATION

I0889387

CPRP

Exam Secrets Study Guide

DEAR FUTURE EXAM SUCCESS STORY

First of all, **THANK YOU** for purchasing Mometrix study materials!

Second, congratulations! You are one of the few determined test-takers who are committed to doing whatever it takes to excel on your exam. **You have come to the right place.** We developed these study materials with one goal in mind: to deliver you the information you need in a format that's concise and easy to use.

In addition to optimizing your guide for the content of the test, we've outlined our recommended steps for breaking down the preparation process into small, attainable goals so you can make sure you stay on track.

We've also analyzed the entire test-taking process, identifying the most common pitfalls and showing how you can overcome them and be ready for any curveball the test throws you.

Standardized testing is one of the biggest obstacles on your road to success, which only increases the importance of doing well in the high-pressure, high-stakes environment of test day. Your results on this test could have a significant impact on your future, and this guide provides the information and practical advice to help you achieve your full potential on test day.

Your success is our success

We would love to hear from you! If you would like to share the story of your exam success or if you have any questions or comments in regard to our products, please contact us at **800-673-8175** or **support@mometrix.com**.

Thanks again for your business and we wish you continued success!

Sincerely,
The Mometrix Test Preparation Team

Need more help? Check out our flashcards at:
http://mometrixflashcards.com/CPRP

Written and edited by the Mometrix Exam Secrets Test Prep Team
Printed in the United States of America

Table of Contents

Introduction

Thank you for purchasing this resource! You have made the choice to prepare yourself for a test that could have a huge impact on your future, and this guide is designed to help you be fully ready for test day. Obviously, it's important to have a solid understanding of the test material, but you also need to be prepared for the unique environment and stressors of the test, so that you can perform to the best of your abilities.

For this purpose, the first section that appears in this guide is the **Secret Keys**. We've devoted countless hours to meticulously researching what works and what doesn't, and we've boiled down our findings to the five most impactful steps you can take to improve your performance on the test. We start at the beginning with study planning and move through the preparation process, all the way to the testing strategies that will help you get the most out of what you know when you're finally sitting in front of the test.

We recommend that you start preparing for your test as far in advance as possible. However, if you've bought this guide as a last-minute study resource and only have a few days before your test, we recommend that you skip over the first two Secret Keys since they address a long-term study plan.

If you struggle with **test anxiety**, we strongly encourage you to check out our recommendations for how you can overcome it. Test anxiety is a formidable foe, but it can be beaten, and we want to make sure you have the tools you need to defeat it.

Secret Key #1 – Plan Big, Study Small

There's a lot riding on your performance. If you want to ace this test, you're going to need to keep your skills sharp and the material fresh in your mind. You need a plan that lets you review everything you need to know while still fitting in your schedule. We'll break this strategy down into three categories.

Information Organization

Start with the information you already have: the official test outline. From this, you can make a complete list of all the concepts you need to cover before the test. Organize these concepts into groups that can be studied together, and create a list of any related vocabulary you need to learn so you can brush up on any difficult terms. You'll want to keep this vocabulary list handy once you actually start studying since you may need to add to it along the way.

Time Management

Once you have your set of study concepts, decide how to spread them out over the time you have left before the test. Break your study plan into small, clear goals so you have a manageable task for each day and know exactly what you're doing. Then just focus on one small step at a time. When you manage your time this way, you don't need to spend hours at a time studying. Studying a small block of content for a short period each day helps you retain information better and avoid stressing over how much you have left to do. You can relax knowing that you have a plan to cover everything in time. In order for this strategy to be effective though, you have to start studying early and stick to your schedule. Avoid the exhaustion and futility that comes from last-minute cramming!

Study Environment

The environment you study in has a big impact on your learning. Studying in a coffee shop, while probably more enjoyable, is not likely to be as fruitful as studying in a quiet room. It's important to keep distractions to a minimum. You're only planning to study for a short block of time, so make the most of it. Don't pause to check your phone or get up to find a snack. It's also important to **avoid multitasking**. Research has consistently shown that multitasking will make your studying dramatically less effective. Your study area should also be comfortable and well-lit so you don't have the distraction of straining your eyes or sitting on an uncomfortable chair.

The time of day you study is also important. You want to be rested and alert. Don't wait until just before bedtime. Study when you'll be most likely to comprehend and remember. Even better, if you know what time of day your test will be, set that time aside for study. That way your brain will be used to working on that subject at that specific time and you'll have a better chance of recalling information.

Finally, it can be helpful to team up with others who are studying for the same test. Your actual studying should be done in as isolated an environment as possible, but the work of organizing the information and setting up the study plan can be divided up. In between study sessions, you can discuss with your teammates the concepts that you're all studying and quiz each other on the details. Just be sure that your teammates are as serious about the test as you are. If you find that your study time is being replaced with social time, you might need to find a new team.

Secret Key #2 – Make Your Studying Count

You're devoting a lot of time and effort to preparing for this test, so you want to be absolutely certain it will pay off. This means doing more than just reading the content and hoping you can remember it on test day. It's important to make every minute of study count. There are two main areas you can focus on to make your studying count.

Retention

It doesn't matter how much time you study if you can't remember the material. You need to make sure you are retaining the concepts. To check your retention of the information you're learning, try recalling it at later times with minimal prompting. Try carrying around flashcards and glance at one or two from time to time or ask a friend who's also studying for the test to quiz you.

To enhance your retention, look for ways to put the information into practice so that you can apply it rather than simply recalling it. If you're using the information in practical ways, it will be much easier to remember. Similarly, it helps to solidify a concept in your mind if you're not only reading it to yourself but also explaining it to someone else. Ask a friend to let you teach them about a concept you're a little shaky on (or speak aloud to an imaginary audience if necessary). As you try to summarize, define, give examples, and answer your friend's questions, you'll understand the concepts better and they will stay with you longer. Finally, step back for a big picture view and ask yourself how each piece of information fits with the whole subject. When you link the different concepts together and see them working together as a whole, it's easier to remember the individual components.

Finally, practice showing your work on any multi-step problems, even if you're just studying. Writing out each step you take to solve a problem will help solidify the process in your mind, and you'll be more likely to remember it during the test.

Modality

Modality simply refers to the means or method by which you study. Choosing a study modality that fits your own individual learning style is crucial. No two people learn best in exactly the same way, so it's important to know your strengths and use them to your advantage.

For example, if you learn best by visualization, focus on visualizing a concept in your mind and draw an image or a diagram. Try color-coding your notes, illustrating them, or creating symbols that will trigger your mind to recall a learned concept. If you learn best by hearing or discussing information, find a study partner who learns the same way or read aloud to yourself. Think about how to put the information in your own words. Imagine that you are giving a lecture on the topic and record yourself so you can listen to it later.

For any learning style, flashcards can be helpful. Organize the information so you can take advantage of spare moments to review. Underline key words or phrases. Use different colors for different categories. Mnemonic devices (such as creating a short list in which every item starts with the same letter) can also help with retention. Find what works best for you and use it to store the information in your mind most effectively and easily.

Secret Key #3 – Practice the Right Way

Your success on test day depends not only on how many hours you put into preparing, but also on whether you prepared the right way. It's good to check along the way to see if your studying is paying off. One of the most effective ways to do this is by taking practice tests to evaluate your progress. Practice tests are useful because they show exactly where you need to improve. Every time you take a practice test, pay special attention to these three groups of questions:

- The questions you got wrong
- The questions you had to guess on, even if you guessed right
- The questions you found difficult or slow to work through

This will show you exactly what your weak areas are, and where you need to devote more study time. Ask yourself why each of these questions gave you trouble. Was it because you didn't understand the material? Was it because you didn't remember the vocabulary? Do you need more repetitions on this type of question to build speed and confidence? Dig into those questions and figure out how you can strengthen your weak areas as you go back to review the material.

Additionally, many practice tests have a section explaining the answer choices. It can be tempting to read the explanation and think that you now have a good understanding of the concept. However, an explanation likely only covers part of the question's broader context. Even if the explanation makes perfect sense, **go back and investigate** every concept related to the question until you're positive you have a thorough understanding.

As you go along, keep in mind that the practice test is just that: practice. Memorizing these questions and answers will not be very helpful on the actual test because it is unlikely to have any of the same exact questions. If you only know the right answers to the sample questions, you won't be prepared for the real thing. **Study the concepts** until you understand them fully, and then you'll be able to answer any question that shows up on the test.

It's important to wait on the practice tests until you're ready. If you take a test on your first day of study, you may be overwhelmed by the amount of material covered and how much you need to learn. Work up to it gradually.

On test day, you'll need to be prepared for answering questions, managing your time, and using the test-taking strategies you've learned. It's a lot to balance, like a mental marathon that will have a big impact on your future. Like training for a marathon, you'll need to start slowly and work your way up. When test day arrives, you'll be ready.

Start with the strategies you've read in the first two Secret Keys—plan your course and study in the way that works best for you. If you have time, consider using multiple study resources to get different approaches to the same concepts. It can be helpful to see difficult concepts from more than one angle. Then find a good source for practice tests. Many times, the test website will suggest potential study resources or provide sample tests.

Practice Test Strategy

If you're able to find at least three practice tests, we recommend this strategy:

Untimed and Open-Book Practice

Take the first test with no time constraints and with your notes and study guide handy. Take your time and focus on applying the strategies you've learned.

Timed and Open-Book Practice

Take the second practice test open-book as well, but set a timer and practice pacing yourself to finish in time.

Timed and Closed-Book Practice

Take any other practice tests as if it were test day. Set a timer and put away your study materials. Sit at a table or desk in a quiet room, imagine yourself at the testing center, and answer questions as quickly and accurately as possible.

Keep repeating timed and closed-book tests on a regular basis until you run out of practice tests or it's time for the actual test. Your mind will be ready for the schedule and stress of test day, and you'll be able to focus on recalling the material you've learned.

Secret Key #4 – Pace Yourself

Once you're fully prepared for the material on the test, your biggest challenge on test day will be managing your time. Just knowing that the clock is ticking can make you panic even if you have plenty of time left. Work on pacing yourself so you can build confidence against the time constraints of the exam. Pacing is a difficult skill to master, especially in a high-pressure environment, so **practice is vital**.

Set time expectations for your pace based on how much time is available. For example, if a section has 60 questions and the time limit is 30 minutes, you know you have to average 30 seconds or less per question in order to answer them all. Although 30 seconds is the hard limit, set 25 seconds per question as your goal, so you reserve extra time to spend on harder questions. When you budget extra time for the harder questions, you no longer have any reason to stress when those questions take longer to answer.

Don't let this time expectation distract you from working through the test at a calm, steady pace, but keep it in mind so you don't spend too much time on any one question. Recognize that taking extra time on one question you don't understand may keep you from answering two that you do understand later in the test. If your time limit for a question is up and you're still not sure of the answer, mark it and move on, and come back to it later if the time and the test format allow. If the testing format doesn't allow you to return to earlier questions, just make an educated guess; then put it out of your mind and move on.

On the easier questions, be careful not to rush. It may seem wise to hurry through them so you have more time for the challenging ones, but it's not worth missing one if you know the concept and just didn't take the time to read the question fully. Work efficiently but make sure you understand the question and have looked at all of the answer choices, since more than one may seem right at first.

Even if you're paying attention to the time, you may find yourself a little behind at some point. You should speed up to get back on track, but do so wisely. Don't panic; just take a few seconds less on each question until you're caught up. Don't guess without thinking, but do look through the answer choices and eliminate any you know are wrong. If you can get down to two choices, it is often worthwhile to guess from those. Once you've chosen an answer, move on and don't dwell on any that you skipped or had to hurry through. If a question was taking too long, chances are it was one of the harder ones, so you weren't as likely to get it right anyway.

On the other hand, if you find yourself getting ahead of schedule, it may be beneficial to slow down a little. The more quickly you work, the more likely you are to make a careless mistake that will affect your score. You've budgeted time for each question, so don't be afraid to spend that time. Practice an efficient but careful pace to get the most out of the time you have.

Secret Key #5 – Have a Plan for Guessing

When you're taking the test, you may find yourself stuck on a question. Some of the answer choices seem better than others, but you don't see the one answer choice that is obviously correct. What do you do?

The scenario described above is very common, yet most test takers have not effectively prepared for it. Developing and practicing a plan for guessing may be one of the single most effective uses of your time as you get ready for the exam.

In developing your plan for guessing, there are three questions to address:

- When should you start the guessing process?
- How should you narrow down the choices?
- Which answer should you choose?

When to Start the Guessing Process

Unless your plan for guessing is to select C every time (which, despite its merits, is not what we recommend), you need to leave yourself enough time to apply your answer elimination strategies. Since you have a limited amount of time for each question, that means that if you're going to give yourself the best shot at guessing correctly, you have to decide quickly whether or not you will guess.

Of course, the best-case scenario is that you don't have to guess at all, so first, see if you can answer the question based on your knowledge of the subject and basic reasoning skills. Focus on the key words in the question and try to jog your memory of related topics. Give yourself a chance to bring the knowledge to mind, but once you realize that you don't have (or you can't access) the knowledge you need to answer the question, it's time to start the guessing process.

It's almost always better to start the guessing process too early than too late. It only takes a few seconds to remember something and answer the question from knowledge. Carefully eliminating wrong answer choices takes longer. Plus, going through the process of eliminating answer choices can actually help jog your memory.

Summary: Start the guessing process as soon as you decide that you can't answer the question based on your knowledge.

How to Narrow Down the Choices

The next chapter in this book (**Test-Taking Strategies**) includes a wide range of strategies for how to approach questions and how to look for answer choices to eliminate. You will definitely want to read those carefully, practice them, and figure out which ones work best for you. Here though, we're going to address a mindset rather than a particular strategy.

Your odds of guessing an answer correctly depend on how many options you are choosing from.

Number of options left	5	4	3	2	1
Odds of guessing correctly	20%	25%	33%	50%	100%

You can see from this chart just how valuable it is to be able to eliminate incorrect answers and make an educated guess, but there are two things that many test takers do that cause them to miss out on the benefits of guessing:

- Accidentally eliminating the correct answer
- Selecting an answer based on an impression

We'll look at the first one here, and the second one in the next section.

To avoid accidentally eliminating the correct answer, we recommend a thought exercise called **the $5 challenge**. In this challenge, you only eliminate an answer choice from contention if you are willing to bet $5 on it being wrong. Why $5? Five dollars is a small but not insignificant amount of money. It's an amount you could afford to lose but wouldn't want to throw away. And while losing $5 once might not hurt too much, doing it twenty times will set you back $100. In the same way, each small decision you make—eliminating a choice here, guessing on a question there—won't by itself impact your score very much, but when you put them all together, they can make a big difference. By holding each answer choice elimination decision to a higher standard, you can reduce the risk of accidentally eliminating the correct answer.

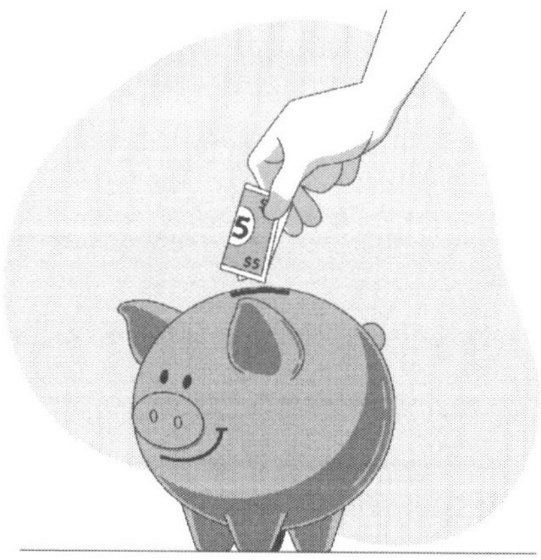

The $5 challenge can also be applied in a positive sense: If you are willing to bet $5 that an answer choice *is* correct, go ahead and mark it as correct.

Summary: Only eliminate an answer choice if you are willing to bet $5 that it is wrong.

Which Answer to Choose

You're taking the test. You've run into a hard question and decided you'll have to guess. You've eliminated all the answer choices you're willing to bet $5 on. Now you have to pick an answer. Why do we even need to talk about this? Why can't you just pick whichever one you feel like when the time comes?

The answer to these questions is that if you don't come into the test with a plan, you'll rely on your impression to select an answer choice, and if you do that, you risk falling into a trap. The test writers know that everyone who takes their test will be guessing on some of the questions, so they intentionally write wrong answer choices to seem plausible. You still have to pick an answer though, and if the wrong answer choices are designed to look right, how can you ever be sure that you're not falling for their trap? The best solution we've found to this dilemma is to take the decision out of your hands entirely. Here is the process we recommend:

Once you've eliminated any choices that you are confident (willing to bet $5) are wrong, select the first remaining choice as your answer.

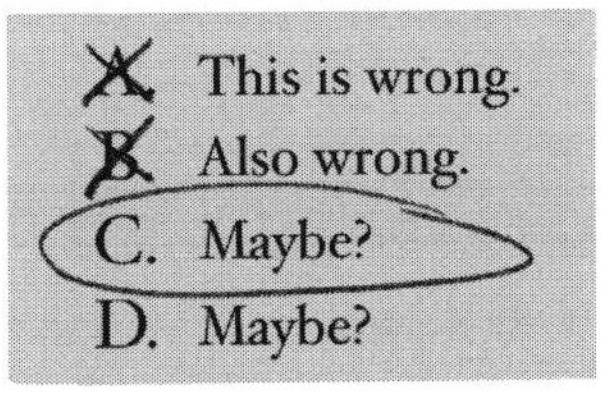

Whether you choose to select the first remaining choice, the second, or the last, the important thing is that you use some preselected standard. Using this approach guarantees that you will not be enticed into selecting an answer choice that looks right, because you are not basing your decision on how the answer choices look.

This is not meant to make you question your knowledge. Instead, it is to help you recognize the difference between your knowledge and your impressions. There's a huge difference between thinking an answer is right because of what you know, and thinking an answer is right because it looks or sounds like it should be right.

Summary: To ensure that your selection is appropriately random, make a predetermined selection from among all answer choices you have not eliminated.

Test-Taking Strategies

This section contains a list of test-taking strategies that you may find helpful as you work through the test. By taking what you know and applying logical thought, you can maximize your chances of answering any question correctly!

It is very important to realize that every question is different and every person is different: no single strategy will work on every question, and no single strategy will work for every person. That's why we've included all of them here, so you can try them out and determine which ones work best for different types of questions and which ones work best for you.

Question Strategies

✓ Read Carefully

Read the question and the answer choices carefully. Don't miss the question because you misread the terms. You have plenty of time to read each question thoroughly and make sure you understand what is being asked. Yet a happy medium must be attained, so don't waste too much time. You must read carefully and efficiently.

✓ Contextual Clues

Look for contextual clues. If the question includes a word you are not familiar with, look at the immediate context for some indication of what the word might mean. Contextual clues can often give you all the information you need to decipher the meaning of an unfamiliar word. Even if you can't determine the meaning, you may be able to narrow down the possibilities enough to make a solid guess at the answer to the question.

✓ Prefixes

If you're having trouble with a word in the question or answer choices, try dissecting it. Take advantage of every clue that the word might include. Prefixes can be a huge help. Usually, they allow you to determine a basic meaning. *Pre-* means before, *post-* means after, *pro-* is positive, *de-* is negative. From prefixes, you can get an idea of the general meaning of the word and try to put it into context.

✓ Hedge Words

Watch out for critical hedge words, such as *likely, may, can, often, almost, mostly, usually, generally, rarely,* and *sometimes.* Question writers insert these hedge phrases to cover every possibility. Often an answer choice will be wrong simply because it leaves no room for exception. Be on guard for answer choices that have definitive words such as *exactly* and *always.*

✓ Switchback Words

Stay alert for *switchbacks.* These are the words and phrases frequently used to alert you to shifts in thought. The most common switchback words are *but, although,* and *however.* Others include *nevertheless, on the other hand, even though, while, in spite of, despite,* and *regardless of.* Switchback words are important to catch because they can change the direction of the question or an answer choice.

✓ Face Value

When in doubt, use common sense. Accept the situation in the problem at face value. Don't read too much into it. These problems will not require you to make wild assumptions. If you have to go beyond creativity and warp time or space in order to have an answer choice fit the question, then you should move on and consider the other answer choices. These are normal problems rooted in reality. The applicable relationship or explanation may not be readily apparent, but it is there for you to figure out. Use your common sense to interpret anything that isn't clear.

Answer Choice Strategies

✓ Answer Selection

The most thorough way to pick an answer choice is to identify and eliminate wrong answers until only one is left, then confirm it is the correct answer. Sometimes an answer choice may immediately seem right, but be careful. The test writers will usually put more than one reasonable answer choice on each question, so take a second to read all of them and make sure that the other choices are not equally obvious. As long as you have time left, it is better to read every answer choice than to pick the first one that looks right without checking the others.

✓ Answer Choice Families

An answer choice family consists of two (in rare cases, three) answer choices that are very similar in construction and cannot all be true at the same time. If you see two answer choices that are direct opposites or parallels, one of them is usually the correct answer. For instance, if one answer choice says that quantity *x* increases and another either says that quantity *x* decreases (opposite) or says that quantity *y* increases (parallel), then those answer choices would fall into the same family. An answer choice that doesn't match the construction of the answer choice family is more likely to be incorrect. Most questions will not have answer choice families, but when they do appear, you should be prepared to recognize them.

✓ Eliminate Answers

Eliminate answer choices as soon as you realize they are wrong, but make sure you consider all possibilities. If you are eliminating answer choices and realize that the last one you are left with is also wrong, don't panic. Start over and consider each choice again. There may be something you missed the first time that you will realize on the second pass.

✓ Avoid Fact Traps

Don't be distracted by an answer choice that is factually true but doesn't answer the question. You are looking for the choice that answers the question. Stay focused on what the question is asking for so you don't accidentally pick an answer that is true but incorrect. Always go back to the question and make sure the answer choice you've selected actually answers the question and is not merely a true statement.

✓ Extreme Statements

In general, you should avoid answers that put forth extreme actions as standard practice or proclaim controversial ideas as established fact. An answer choice that states the "process should be used in certain situations, if..." is much more likely to be correct than one that states the "process should be discontinued completely." The first is a calm rational statement and doesn't even make a definitive, uncompromising stance, using a hedge word *if* to provide wiggle room, whereas the second choice is far more extreme.

⊘ BENCHMARK

As you read through the answer choices and you come across one that seems to answer the question well, mentally select that answer choice. This is not your final answer, but it's the one that will help you evaluate the other answer choices. The one that you selected is your benchmark or standard for judging each of the other answer choices. Every other answer choice must be compared to your benchmark. That choice is correct until proven otherwise by another answer choice beating it. If you find a better answer, then that one becomes your new benchmark. Once you've decided that no other choice answers the question as well as your benchmark, you have your final answer.

⊘ PREDICT THE ANSWER

Before you even start looking at the answer choices, it is often best to try to predict the answer. When you come up with the answer on your own, it is easier to avoid distractions and traps because you will know exactly what to look for. The right answer choice is unlikely to be word-for-word what you came up with, but it should be a close match. Even if you are confident that you have the right answer, you should still take the time to read each option before moving on.

General Strategies

⊘ TOUGH QUESTIONS

If you are stumped on a problem or it appears too hard or too difficult, don't waste time. Move on! Remember though, if you can quickly check for obviously incorrect answer choices, your chances of guessing correctly are greatly improved. Before you completely give up, at least try to knock out a couple of possible answers. Eliminate what you can and then guess at the remaining answer choices before moving on.

⊘ CHECK YOUR WORK

Since you will probably not know every term listed and the answer to every question, it is important that you get credit for the ones that you do know. Don't miss any questions through careless mistakes. If at all possible, try to take a second to look back over your answer selection and make sure you've selected the correct answer choice and haven't made a costly careless mistake (such as marking an answer choice that you didn't mean to mark). This quick double check should more than pay for itself in caught mistakes for the time it costs.

⊘ PACE YOURSELF

It's easy to be overwhelmed when you're looking at a page full of questions; your mind is confused and full of random thoughts, and the clock is ticking down faster than you would like. Calm down and maintain the pace that you have set for yourself. Especially as you get down to the last few minutes of the test, don't let the small numbers on the clock make you panic. As long as you are on track by monitoring your pace, you are guaranteed to have time for each question.

☑ Don't Rush

It is very easy to make errors when you are in a hurry. Maintaining a fast pace in answering questions is pointless if it makes you miss questions that you would have gotten right otherwise. Test writers like to include distracting information and wrong answers that seem right. Taking a little extra time to avoid careless mistakes can make all the difference in your test score. Find a pace that allows you to be confident in the answers that you select.

☑ Keep Moving

Panicking will not help you pass the test, so do your best to stay calm and keep moving. Taking deep breaths and going through the answer elimination steps you practiced can help to break through a stress barrier and keep your pace.

Final Notes

The combination of a solid foundation of content knowledge and the confidence that comes from practicing your plan for applying that knowledge is the key to maximizing your performance on test day. As your foundation of content knowledge is built up and strengthened, you'll find that the strategies included in this chapter become more and more effective in helping you quickly sift through the distractions and traps of the test to isolate the correct answer.

Now that you're preparing to move forward into the test content chapters of this book, be sure to keep your goal in mind. As you read, think about how you will be able to apply this information on the test. If you've already seen sample questions for the test and you have an idea of the question format and style, try to come up with questions of your own that you can answer based on what you're reading. This will give you valuable practice applying your knowledge in the same ways you can expect to on test day.

Good luck and good studying!

Interpersonal Competencies

PsyR

Psychiatric rehabilitation, commonly referred to as PsyR, is the practice of assisting mentally ill people in coping with, adjusting to, or overcoming the symptoms of their diseases so that they can function in society. Professionals in this field help individuals establish and reach goals to cope with their illnesses. This can include overcoming physical limitations, loss of skills or abilities, cognitive malfunction, social concerns, medication side effects, stigma associated with disease, loss of self-confidence, and much more. The ultimate goal of PsyR is for the client to once again be able to live independently, function in society, interact with others, and live life to the fullest. The range of tasks can be as small as maintaining personal hygiene or as major as driving a car, holding a job, and dating.

Principles of PsyR

Individualization of services – All areas of psychiatric rehabilitation should be specifically designed for each individual. This includes assessment, setting goals, and designing and providing services. This principle should be followed even in a group setting.

Maximum client involvement – Individuals should be involved to the greatest extent possible in developing their own goals and plans for rehabilitation and recovery. This includes providing individuals with all choices and paying careful attention to their preferences, values, and long term plans. Plans designed only by professionals for their clients will have a low rate of success.

Normalized and community-based services – Normalization means being a part of accepted societal roles and values. Examples would be functioning as an employee, a neighbor or colleague, a student, or even a parent. Services should allow individuals to lead normal lives in regards to housing, shopping, working, community activities, and all other aspects of life.

Strengths focus – Emphasis should be placed on utilizing or building on an individual's strengths instead of highlighting weaknesses or deficiencies.

Situational assessments – Overall or global evaluations do not give a good picture of individuals in their unique environment or situation. Individuals should be evaluated in situations that are specific to their unique needs and personal goals to give a clear understanding of progress.

Holistic, integrated approach to treatment and rehabilitation – It best serves the individual for the process of treating his illness and the process of rehabilitation, are unified and concurrent. The two approaches can complement each other and greatly improve the chance for recovery and successful goal achievement.

Ongoing, coordinated, accessible services – Psychiatric rehabilitation should be a service that individuals with mental illness can receive at any time and for as long as needed during their lifetimes. Related programs should be set up so that they are easy to use and receive and do not duplicated each other's efforts

Vocational focus – Working is a big part of people's lives and all people who want to work should have the opportunity. Individuals should have resources to develop skills and find work at which they can succeed.

Skills training – Individuals should have access to education or training that helps them reach their goals and function in their unique settings.

Environmental modifications – Individuals should have assistance in making any needed changes to their unique environments to improve quality of life, reach goals, and achieve success.

Partnership with the Family – With the consent of mentally ill individuals, their families should be fully informed, educated, and recruited into the support of their relative.

Assessment and outcome-based focus – Individuals and outcomes should be continuously analyzed to make sure each person receives needed services, services are appropriate, and entire systems are working efficiently.

Qualities of an Ideal Program

- Individual choice in creating goals, picking the setting, and levels of support should be a top priority
- All aspects of the program should be tailored to the needs of each individual
- All services and support provided should naturally match the environment for optimal normalization
- No limit should be placed on the amount or duration of support creating a system that meets the changing needs of the individual
- Individuals should be shown respect and treated with dignity in all aspects of the program including confidentiality
- All support staff and program characteristics should clearly show confidence in the ability of individuals to reach their goals

PsyR Values

Person-orientation – Emphasis is placed on building relationships with individual people rather than focusing on a certain diagnosis or disease. This means that rehabilitation plans are built around the specific needs of the individual and not mass produced to fit typical illness course, symptoms, and outcomes.

Functioning – Emphasis is placed on helping people perform better in their lives. Rehabilitation is not about treating symptoms or curing illness; it is about managing life.

Support – Emphasis is placed giving individuals all the help they need and desire for an unlimited time period. Individuals should know that support will be there when needed and the level and duration are guided by them.

Environmental Specificity – Emphasis is placed on providing support and training to people in their chosen environment. This means rehabilitation happens within the community and involves working with individuals at their residence, on the job, and where they play. This is an important concept of PsyR because people respond differently in different environments, requiring different levels and types of support.

Involvement – This core belief of PsyR makes the involvement of those receiving services crucial. Clients should take an active role in all aspects of rehabilitation including setting goals, developing a plan, helping create programs, and determining outcome measures. Rehabilitation should be seen as a cooperative effort between the practitioner and client.

Choice – Emphasis is placed on self-determination. The client's desires and needs should drive all decisions. Once client choices have been made, practitioners provide needed support, training, and assistance.

Outcome-orientation – All services and assistance are designed to achieving a specific outcome. Outcomes and outcome measures are determined by client goals and choices.

Potential for Growth – Emphasis is placed on the belief that every individual can grow. Practitioners work from the perspective that clients can achieve the goals they set, become productive members of the community, and live meaningful, fulfilling lives.

Responsibilities of PsyR Professionals

- PsyR professionals should make individuals receiving rehabilitation services their main priority.
- PsyR professionals should not maintain any other type of relationship with an individual who is receiving services from them.
- PsyR professionals should always exhibit integrity when dealing with other professionals, agencies and organizations, family members, domestic partners, and all other resource individuals so that these people can help their clients as much as possible.
- PsyR professionals should always respect and encourage clients' full involvement in decision making about all aspects of services.
- PsyR professionals should value the privacy of their clients and keep all information confidential.
- PsyR professionals should treat other professional colleagues fairly and with consideration and respect.

Skills Training

- The purpose is developing skills
- The focus is on treating by teaching
- Emphasis is on identifying skills that an individual needs for their desired environment
- Cycle of Tell, Show, and Do is used to build skills
- Feedback is given about strengths and weaknesses in a positive approach
- Obstacles to success are identified and a plan developed to overcome them

Schizophrenia

Positive symptoms are effects of illness or disease that are added to normal experiences or behavior. The most common of these symptoms are delusions. Suffers become convinced about ideas that are not true, often described as losing touch with reality. Delusions can often include paranoid thoughts such as being controlled or watched by others or fantasy beliefs about one's own abilities, possessions, or life. Hallucinations are also common symptoms in which sufferers see, hear, or experiences things that do not exist. This often takes the form of hearing voices which might range from simply annoying to instructing the sufferer to commit violence. Thought disorders are another positive symptom in which the individual has trouble with cognitive functions or processing information.

Negative symptoms are normal things lost or lessened due to schizophrenia. Avolition is a common symptom in which a person loses their drive or will power. Anhedonia is similar in that people also lose their will or desire to do things that are fun or enjoyable. These two symptoms cause suffers to avoid friends and family and fail to complete life tasks such as job requirements, paying bills, and maintaining a home. People with schizophrenia often experience a loss of emotional expression, commonly known as flat affect. This term comes from the appearance of a complete lack of emotion. Another symptom commonly experienced is the loss of smooth speech and clear thought processes. This makes it difficult and frustrating for the sufferer to interact with others and sustain conversations.

Schizophrenia begins with the prodromal phase. This is a stage where the individual starts to experience both positive and negative symptoms. During this time normal function begins to break down. The second phase is the active stage, also known as the acute phase. This is the most severe period of the disorder. Symptoms will be most noticeable and disruptive of life functions. The third and final phase is referred to as residual. During this time, the severity of symptoms starts to decrease. Although both positive and negative symptoms will lessen, negative symptoms such as loss of motivation, focus, and emotion are likely to continue. These stages of the disease are likely to repeat frequently during a person's lifetime.

Schizophrenia is a mental illness that is also sometimes referred to as a communication disorder. The disruption in communication can be profound. Due to the experiencing of hallucinations and delusions as well as experiencing a thought disorder, an individual with schizophrenia may not make sense when he speaks. Comments might appear as gibberish or a string of unrelated statements. Comments might also be bizarre in nature or statements can stop mid thought with no ability to recapture the remaining information. Individuals with schizophrenia sometimes go for several hours without speaking or appearing to hear others who speak to them. Individuals with schizophrenia suffer cognitive impairment with affects their ability to focus while communicating as well as their ability to remember or recall what was said.

Major Depressive Episode Criteria

At least five or more of the following symptoms should be exhibited during a two-week period in a manner that is different from the person's normal functioning in order to diagnose a major depressive episode:

- A depressed mood daily or almost daily – can be reported by the individual or noticed by other people
- A loss of interest or enjoyment in daily activities or interactions – can be reported by the individual or noticed by other people
- A significant change in weight with no other explanation
- Difficulty sleeping or sleeping for extensive periods every day
- Excessive motion or severely limited motion as noticed by others
- Extreme fatigue or lack of energy every day
- A sense or poor self-worth or overwhelming, misplaced guilt
- Cognitive difficulty exhibited in problems concentrating, making decisions, or processing information
- Suicidal thoughts or actions or a focus on dying

Dual Diagnosis

Dual diagnosis refers to an individual recognized to have a mental illness as well as a separate condition. Most commonly the second condition is either a substance abuse problem or a developmental disability. Substance abuse can come before the mental illness begins or be a result of an individual trying to combat psychiatric symptoms of his illness. Mental health providers should be prepared to treat both conditions and not ignore the substance abuse. Developmental disabilities such as intellectual disability, autism, or brain injury can also co-exist with mental illnesses. Since the developmental disability is often apparent and consuming, mental illness may go unnoticed and untreated. Communication difficulties may interfere with a diagnosis. Mental health professionals should be very aware of this problem and give careful consideration to treatment, including medication.

Common Medications

There are several classes of medications used in the treatment of major mental illness. These include antipsychotics for schizophrenia and sometimes manic episodes common with certain mood disorders. Neuroleptic drugs might also be used. In the treatment of major depression, serotonin reuptake inhibitors and tri-cyclic antidepressants are the most common choices. These drugs are also used to treat certain symptoms of both schizophrenia and mood disorders. For bipolar and other mood disorders, mood stabilizers are the most common treatment. Some specific examples include:

- Schizophrenia – Haldol - Risperidol - Clozaril - Zyprexa - Geodon
- Major depression – Tofranil - Prozac - Paxil - Ativan - Zoloft - Effexor
- Bipolar/Mood – Lithobid - Lithium - Valproate - Zyprexa - Geodon

Family Members of Afflicted

Burdens Placed on Family

Objective burdens are those challenges that can easily be identified and labeled. Families with members experiencing ongoing psychiatric disabilities often experience similar burdens including financial difficulties related to the cost of medical care and supporting an individual who cannot work or provide for himself. Other objective burdens are the limits placed on family members' participation in outside activities such as recreation, socialization, hobbies, fitness, or travel. Some family members are burdened by the changing relationship that occurs due to the dependence of the individual with mental illness. How a family operates on a daily basis must change dramatically, often causing dysfunctional and chaotic situations. Some family members might be required to make sacrifices in their careers in order to care for the individual with mental illness.

Subjective burdens are those related to the emotional and mental turmoil family member's experience. Family members may have different perceptions about the burden that they are experiencing. The primary care provider in the family might be well adjusted to the challenges while another member who has less of a burden might perceive it as more. This perception can be directly tied to the amount of disturbance in normal activities and pursuits. Another area of subjective burden can be situations and decisions that force family members to take oppositional positions. This could be decisions regarding medical care, law enforcement involvement, and involuntary commitment proceedings. Family relationships can become permanently altered, family members might become estranged, and marriages can end in divorce, as a result.

Behaviors That Increase Burden

- Behaviors that are hateful, antagonistic, harmful to others, or violent
- Paranoia or delusions related to family members
- Wide variations in moods resulting in inconsistent responses and unexpected behaviors
- Behavior or actions in public that are embarrassing to other family members or shocking and repugnant to others
- Complete lack of motivation that others perceive as laziness or playing up the illness to avoid work or obligations
- Behavior that is damaging to oneself such as failing to maintain personal hygiene by bathing, brushing teeth, and maintaining appearances
- Behavior that is damaging to one's life such as mismanagement of financial affairs, irresponsibility with money, and destruction or abandonment of personal property

Levels of Family Involvement

A first-tier family member is someone in the immediate family who usually lives with the individual with mental illness. This person has taken on the responsibility of being the main person to provide care for that individual. In most cases this is one person, however it could be several. Most often the first-tier family member is female, commonly the wife, mother, or daughter of that individual. This person carries the largest burden in the family, with a daily life consumed by caring for the individual with mental illness. This person functions as nurse, scheduler, supervisor, and mediator with the other family members. He or she often tries to mitigate the effects of the illness on other family members. Little if any time is available for personal activities and abandonment of a job or career might be necessary. When not directly caring for the individual with mental illness, this family member is consumed by thoughts related to him or her.

A second-tier family member might live with the individual with mental illness or close by. These family members are affected by the illness, but on a lesser level than the first-tier members. There is often a greater fear of crisis moments or relapses among members at this level. Their daily life might experience minimal impact, but crisis or relapse intrudes sharply. In attempts to avoid the challenges related to the individual's mental illness, second tier members might avoid the first-tier members. This can be disruptive to family life in the least and lead to divorce and estrangement at its worst. Occasionally some second-tier members who stay uninvolved on a regular basis may voluntarily take key roles during a crisis or acute stage of illness.

Third tier relatives do not live with the individual with mental illness, but have a strong enough family connection to be concerned with his or her health and wellness. These members are not exposed to the daily challenges experienced by the individual with mental illness and the first and second tier members. Knowledge of the situation might often be second hand and anecdotal. Reactions of family members at this level can vary considerably. Some refuse to believe the individual is sick, suggesting instead the he is just lazy or looking for attention or perhaps he is ill but exaggerating his symptoms. Other members might accept the illness, but feel too distant or uninformed to help in any way. These family members might be quick to place blame on first and second tier members for not solving the problem.

SPECIFIC BURDENS

Spouses

- Unhappiness in the marriage
- Lack of marital support
- Dysfunction in normal marital roles such as sexual partner, provider, homemaker, and confidante
- Economic concerns
- Single parenting
- Lack of social interaction or avoidance of social situations
- Suffering from emotional problems such as situational depression
- Divorce

Children and siblings

- Loss of life experiences or opportunities due to limits placed on the family life
- Abnormal childhood experiences and distorted view of normal behavior and relationships
- Potential for inherited mental illness and emotions associated with this possibility
- Role reversal if a child must serve as a caregiver to a parent
- Overwhelming emotions of fear and uncertainty

Goals for Families

- Practitioners should build a relationship with family members that is a true coalition in order to best help the client
- Practitioners should seek a deep understanding of the family structure and its unique problems and challenges so that sources of stress on the client and his family can be identified
- Practitioners must identify the resources available to and within the family
- Practitioners should analyze what strategies and approaches the family has tried in the past that have worked and what has failed
- The family's strengths should be the foundation of the rehabilitation plan and all training and instruction
- Involve family members in support positions in treatment and rehabilitation for the client by collaborative determination of goals that everyone supports

Survival Skills Workshops

Survival skills workshops can be one day only or include multiple sessions. Topics might include:

- Commonly accepted definitions of the relevant mental illness
- Statistical data regarding the history and occurrence of the disease
- Scientific and medical understanding of the illness
- Details about commonly used medications such as antipsychotics and antidepressants such as side effects, benefits, pharmacology, clinical study data, and effect on recovery
- Possible courses the disease might take and how treatment and rehabilitation can affect that course
- Treatment options available to the individual with mental illness
- Challenges that family members can expect to occur
- Areas of family life and relationships that will be most affected

Suggestions and strategies that families can use to deal with the challenges they encounter such establishing new expectations of the individual and themselves, watching for warning signs of crisis or relapse, and accessing available resources in the community, government, and mental health

Recovery for Family Members

The first phase of family member recovery is first learning of the illness. This phase might be accompanied by denial or an attempt to downplay the diagnosis. An absence of relevant information and inadequate involvement of the mental health professional can further complicate this stage. Family members often experience shock and incredulity. The second phase is accepting the situation and recognizing its potential. Family members at this phase often feel sad and experience hopelessness and grief. The individual might experience a good period, raising hopes, only to crash again. The third phase learning how to deal with the reality of the individual's illness and building the skills necessary to care for him. With professional assistance, families can become very knowledgeable and adept in this role. The final phase is reached by some family members as they recognize the problems inherent in mental health treatment and care. They choose to become advocates for the mentally ill and their families, pushing for changes to the systems and societal misconceptions.

Professional Role Competencies

Principles of Leadership

- Leaders should have a vision that drives all actions and is clearly shared with everyone else
- Leaders should create an overall plan the pulls everyone in the organization together then divides responsibility for the plan appropriately, giving others responsibility
- Leaders should not micromanage
- Leaders should help develop a culture within the organization that identifies the common beliefs, values, and goals and encourages all members to embrace that culture
- Leaders should model expectations yet give other members of the organization the autonomy to challenge themselves and succeed in all areas
- Leaders value the potential and talent of other members and the asset that human expertise can bring to an organization
- Leaders engage other members in all aspects of planning and carryout the organization's mission
- Leaders are continuously learning and seeking new knowledge to embrace change as a requirement for success
- Leaders recognize outstanding members and make them the foundation of the organization

Improving Communication

- Face the individual and keep constant eye contact
- Introduce one idea or thought at a time to the conversation
- Do not rush the communication
- Keep a calm manner at all times
- Exercise patience in all communication
- Listen carefully to the individual's comments taking note of all feelings expressed
- Specifically recognize and confirm the individual's feelings
- If the individual appears not to comprehend your meaning repeat the statement using different words
- Always avoid arguing if possible
- Take time outs if communication breaks down so that you and the individual have time to regroup, return and try again at a later time

Motivational Questioning Techniques

Motivational questioning is used when the practitioner or interviewer recognizes that the individual is conflicted in his feelings toward the substance abuse. Motivational interviewing techniques work with the individual's attitude rather than fighting against it. The interviewer starts by projecting an attitude of empathy for the individual's conflict. The questioning then proceeds with a discussion that analyzes the pros and cons of the situation. The interviewer looks for opportunities to support the individual if he makes statements or asks questions that indicate any motivational inclinations. The interviewer should provide consistent and valuable feedback to the individual throughout the interview to encourage participation and give the sense that change is possible. The interviewer solicits feedback during this discussion and a key element of this technique is maintaining the empathetic and non-judgmental demeanor and tone.

GRACE Strategies

G – Generate a gap between what the individual indicates are his goals and desires and the reality of what is happening

R – Roll with resistance by confirming that the situation has positive and negative aspects; allow the individual to reach his own determinations without forcing him to accept yours

A – Avoid arguing with the individual because forcing will not bring change; allow the individual to move at his own pace

C – "Can do" attitude shows the individual that you are upbeat about the possibilities and certain of his ability to change or accomplish his goals

E – Express empathy for the individual's situation and dilemmas in order to build connections, encourage openness, and emphasize that this is not his fault

Social Learning Theory

Social learning theory is a concept proposed by Albert Bandura in the 1970's, suggesting that people learn by watching other people. In Bandura's theory there are four elements of social learning. The first is attention which is the process of getting the learner to tune in to the source of input. This involves all senses and individual differences influence how easily attention is captured. The second element is retention which is figuring out the coding or break-down of whatever behavior is being observed. The third element is motivation or factors that influence desire to reproduce the observed behavior. Motivation can be intrinsic or extrinsic. The final element is motor reproduction in which the observed behavior is copied. This process is initiated and improved through personal analysis and outside feedback. A person's physical and mental abilities play a key role in his success in copying the observed behavior.

Confidentiality Values

The first value is that of reducing stigma. Mental illness is one of the most stigmatized diseases in the world and stigma can significantly impact and individual's interaction in the community, independence, and productive value to society. Stigma is often accompanied by discrimination, which although prohibited by law, can be further reduced by maintaining confidentiality. The second value is the critical element of developing trust. Treatment and rehabilitation depend on a relationship of mutual trust and respect between practitioner and client. Violating that trust risks the success of treatment, rehabilitation, and recovery. The third value is privacy, something each individual is entitled to. Privacy includes the right to self-determination in all health issues including those related to mental illness. Violations of privacy make an individual less likely to seek treatment or help.

Communication Competence Theory

Communication competence is an individual's skill in utilizing behaviors when communicating, which are most effective and appropriate for that interaction. This is commonly described through a three-part model. The first part is knowledge or simply knowing what behaviors are best in each situation. The second part is skill or being able to effectively engage in the required behaviors. The third part is motivation, or truly having the desire to communicate in a competent manner. All three parts must be present to achieve communication competence. Communication competence is often viewed not just from an individual perspective, but can also be applied to an entire group as an element of the group dynamics.

Interactional View Theory

Interactional view, sometimes known as communication pragmatics, looks at communication from the perspective of a specific situation. The theory holds that all communication is unique to the situation in which it is occurring. Miscommunication occurs when the different viewpoints of those involved interfere with their ability to truly understand one another. Both the relationships among those involved and the content of the communication affect the outcome. This theory is commonly applied to communication within families. Proponents of this theory suggest that communication difficulties can be overcome by rephrasing or restating problems to address differences in perspective and erase misinformation.

Interpersonal Deception Theory

Interpersonal deception theory suggests that individuals are often intentionally deceptive in communications with others. Deceptive messages are divided into three parts. The main message is usually spoken, but is accompanied by verbal or nonverbal secondary elements that give clues about the honesty of the main message. This could include additional dialogue beyond the main message or elements of the delivery such as pauses, stuttering, uncertainty, or choice of words. The third part is non-spoken behaviors such as facial expressions, body movements, and stance, which give further clues about the message. On the other end of communication is a recipient who is on the lookout for dishonesty immediately begins trying to decode the incoming message and its accompanying elements, looking for truth or dishonesty.

Strengths Versus Deficits Models

Strengths Based Models	Deficit Based Models
Focus on a client's abilities, strengths, interests, and preferences	Focus on treating illness and overcoming weaknesses
Client-practitioner relationship is viewed as a partnership	Intense clinical focus directed by professionals
Client's community is viewed as a resource, not a barrier	Often involves isolation from community during treatment
Community resources are emphasized before separate mental health facilities	Use of traditional mental health facilities
Foundation belief in the client's ability to change and grow	Fosters dependency on care providers
Client controls the process	Mental health care providers control the process

Effective Communication Techniques

The diffusing technique is one approach to reducing conflict. Simply agreeing with an angry individual, at least in the beginning, can lessen the conflict. A step just short of agreement is genuine acknowledgment of the validity of another person's viewpoint, even when disagreeing. This allows the communication to move forward in a more positive, less charged atmosphere. Another technique is demonstrating empathy or understanding of another person's ideas and feelings. Thought empathy can be a simple restatement of expressed opinion or feelings to show understanding. Feelings empathy indicates a probable understand of how the other is feeling without imposing what you think they should be feeling. A third technique is known as stroking. This involves finding positive things to say about the other person even in an atmosphere of anger and disagreement. Showing respect improves interpersonal communication. "I" statements are also useful in diffusing conflict. Taking blame or responsibility on some level can lessen the negative feelings of the other person.

Conflict Resolution

The first step in resolving a conflict between individuals is to identify the problem. Each party should participate in open discussion to identify all concerns and give careful attention to the other party's concerns. "I" statements should be used and all language that assigns blame should be avoided. The next step is to brainstorm about possible solutions to the identified problem. All ideas should be mentioned and noted without concern for practicality. The third stage is analyzing each possible solution with each party identify the pros and cons. Compromise might be needed to tailor a solution to serve each party's needs. Once the parties choose a solution, commitment to its success must be mutual. Details must be hammered out covering who does what and when. Continual monitoring of the solution's effectiveness is important for continued harmony and satisfaction for both parties.

Bipolar Disorder

A manic episode is usually diagnosed if an individual maintains an unusually elevated mood is maintained daily for at least one week with three more of the following symptoms:

- Extreme levels of activity or restlessness
- Increased irritability
- Speaking quickly
- Thoughts that speed out of control and are difficult to express verbally
- Difficulty concentrating
- Very short periods of sleep
- Exercising poor judgment
- Spending exorbitant amounts of money
- Increased interest in sex
- Overconfidence in one's capabilities to the point of being unrealistic
- Abuse of alcohol and other substances
- Overly aggressive or sexually overt demeanor
- Refusal to believe something is wrong

Individuals with bipolar disorder usually experience both manic and depressive episodes throughout their lifetimes. Bipolar I disorder describes an individual who have full scale manic episode and depressive episodes. Bipolar II disorder describes an individual who experiences the depressive episodes, but whose manic episodes are much milder in nature, referred to as hypomania. Each individual's episodes follow a unique pattern and frequency. If a person has four or more episodes in one year, the disorder is considered to be rapid-cycling. Avoiding treatment usually exacerbates the illness and produces a decline in health and overall productivity. There is no cure for the disorder and it is a lifetime illness. Although not guaranteed to by symptom free, individuals who seek and follow treatment plans can live productive and somewhat normal lives, suffering fewer and less severe episodes. There is a heredity link increasing the likelihood that siblings and children of those with the illness have a greater chance of developing it.

Typical treatment plans involve both medications and psychosocial treatment. Treatment is most effective when administered and monitored continually be a professional. Medications commonly prescribed include several categories of mood stabilizers which might be taken by the client long term. Lithium is often used as well as anticonvulsants such as Valproate and the newer Topmax and Neurontin. A mental health professional might also prescribe antidepressants during particularly difficult depressive episodes. Clients who are experience sleep disorder are often treated with medications such as Clonazepam, Lorazepam, or the newer Ambien. Individual or group psychotherapy is often recommended as well as family therapy to include those most impacted by the illness. Cognitive therapy might be used to address behaviors common with the disease and psychoeducation can help individuals and their families better understand and cope with the disorder. In extreme cases, especially those with high risk of suicide, electroconvulsive therapy might be attempted.

IAPSRS Code of Ethics

The IAPSRS Code of Ethics mandates that psychiatric rehabilitation professionals keep all client information, disclosures, and records confidential. Confidentiality should only be breeched as is required by law. Confidentiality laws can very by state. If a client needs access to his records, it should be provided promptly. PsyR professionals should be careful never to disclose confidential or identifying information about a client within the records of another client. Maintenance and storage of all client records must be carefully managed so that unauthorized access is not allowed. Professional employees accessing records must be thoroughly trained in confidentiality guidelines. If a PsyR professional wishes to make audio or video recordings of a client, or allow an outside observer, permission must be secured in writing first.

Other principles include:

- All people should have control over their own lives and be able to take part in all decisions that will affect them
- All people should be valued as worthwhile, shown respect, and treated with dignity no matter what disabilities, impairments, or illnesses they might have
- When mental ill people receive psychiatric rehabilitation services, there is hope for improvement and even recovery
- All people can learn new things and grow as individuals
- It is important to be aware of each person's unique personality, needs, culture, ethnicity, and beliefs and show respect for those differences

Intergroup Conflict Theory

Intergroup conflict is an obvious expression of tension between members of a group resulting from a difference in goals, interests, or beliefs. Groups can exist deliberately such as in group therapy, assigned groups for educational purposes, or members of a club or organization. Groups can also exist as a natural state in work environments, family structures, national and cultural unity, and society in general. Some of the major sources of this conflict include competing goals or struggles for resources, desire for power or control, lack of power, cultural differences, need to establish identities, and resisting or seeking assimilation into a larger culture. When intergroup conflict occurs on a larger scale, diversity and cultural boundaries are often involved.

Goals of Psycheducation

- To reach the best outcome for a person with mental illness by supporting a cooperative model of recovery
- To minimize the stress of families by educating them regarding mental illness
- To facilitate coordination of all aspects of treatment and rehabilitation to create a cooperative environment for reaching common goals
- To evaluate and utilize family strengths in the recovery process
- To identify and remedy, if possible, family limitations and deficits
- To support families and the recovery of individuals with mental illness with instruction in coping strategies and problem-solving skills
- To educate families about natural support systems and available community resources
- To recruit family members as equal partners with mental health professionals in the recovery process

Concept of Advocacy

Advocacy is speaking for the rights and needs of the individuals you serve to the people and groups that make decisions affected those individuals. PsyR practitioners can advocate in many areas. The most obvious is with lawmakers on the state and federal level. It is important to have a working relationship with elected representatives who determine funding for various mental health programs. PsyR practitioners should engage in regular communication through letters, emails, or even personal visits. This should be a consolidated effort by numerous individuals and organizations that share similar goals. Lawmakers should be invited to visit facilities and educated on positive benefits of existing programs as well as new areas of need. Since most psychiatric rehabilitation organizations enjoy tax free status, care should be given to follow all applicable laws related to lobbying and political contributions. Tax exempt organizations are limited to a certain amount of lobbying each year and can incur stiff penalties for violations. Such organizations also cannot endorse or make political contributions to candidates. Individuals working for these organizations do not have the same restrictions.

Professional Publications

- Schizophrenia Bulletin
- Psychosocial Rehabilitation Journal
- Psychiatric Services
- Community Mental Health Journal
- American Journal of Psychiatry
- Perspectives in Psychiatric Care
- The Journal of Mental Health Administration

Professional Conferences

<u>International Association of Psychosocial Rehabilitation Services (IAPSRS)</u> – Annual conference in an American or Canadian city and local chapters in more than 40 states offering local meetings, conferences, or support for members.

The World Association for Psychosocial Rehabilitation (WAPR) – Conference every other year at various cities worldwide which draws professionals from all over the globe.

Treatment Options

Biological treatment, also known as somatic treatment, focuses on the use of pharmaceutical drugs to treat mental illness. This includes a wide choice of drugs that fall into the category of antipsychotics, antidepressants, and mood stabilizers. This treatment option is especially common during acute stages of illness and to manage crises. Many studies have proven these options to be effective at eliminating or at least reducing symptoms, especially positive symptoms. Psychosocial treatment can include psychotherapy and other forms of therapy, but in major mental illness, often focuses improving life conditions. This includes focusing on support, altering the individual's environment, and teaching coping skills. This approach can be equally effective. Often treatment involves a combination of both approaches.

Mental Illness/Developmental Disability Treatments

Comprehensive community programs – Facilitates all client education in a real-life environment.

Individualized approaches – Ensures that all education and training meets the needs of a specific individual in their environment.

Train, don't test – Emphasizes ongoing observation and remediation, when needed, to teach skills instead of non-individualized tests that only give a snapshot of that moment.

Unconditional positive approach – Every individual is given absolute respect and not looked down on for lacking skills or ability.

Behavioral communication – Focus on behavior as a key form of communication to give insight into an individual and improve treatment.

Ecological behaviorism –Focus on the complexity of behavior and the influence of environment on behavior.

Balanced approach – Approach which combines both medication and behavioral training to improve an individual's rehabilitation.

Mental Illness/Substance Abuse Treatments

Sequential service model – In this approach, the individual is treated separately and non-concurrently for the two problems. The treating mental health professional decides with condition to treat first after considering his personal beliefs about treatment priorities as well as the severity of each of the problems. This approach has the benefit of using services already available.

Parallel service model – In this approach, the individual is treated for both problems at the same time. Treatment and services come from different programs. Coordination between the two programs is ideal for the best treatment of the individual, but often does not occur. This approach has the benefit of using services already available.

Integrated service model – In this approach, the individual is treated for both problems at the same time. Treatment takes place in a single program in which mental health professionals have been trained to treat both conditions or in which a team of appropriately trained professionals works together. This approach often requires creating new service systems, but is often the best for the individual.

Client-Centered Therapy

Client-centered therapy was first offered by Carl Rogers in the middle of the 1900's. This approach avoids therapist instruction or direction. Instead it focuses on the therapist as a guide to helping a client understand his own unique situation and make positive changes. This requires the development of a relationship of mutual respect and trust. This approach focuses on a positive outlook that says change is possible if the right opportunities are offered within a relationship that is non-judgmental, empathetic, and honest. Therapy often consists of reflection on thoughts and feelings that the therapist has picked up on, but the client is not conscious of. In client-centered therapy, the client is most responsible for his own success.

- Psychiatric rehabilitation professionals should always have the highest standards for their personal behavior in their professional roles.
- PsyR professionals should be knowledgeable and competent in the job they perform.
- PsyR professionals should make their clients' personal needs and desires a priority.
- PsyR professionals should be knowledgeable about, and sensitive to, different cultures in all aspects of their professional work.
- PsyR professionals should support the well-being of our entire society by encouraging the acceptance of individuals with mental illness within the community.

Albert Bandura's Skill Learning

Instruction

An instructor gives specific, step-by-step details on how to complete a task that demonstrates the skill being learned. If the individual is learning how to apply for a job, instructions would include details such as exact language to use when asking for an application, a list of materials needed to complete the application, and appropriate behavior for an interview.

Modeling – Watch someone else using the skill being learned. The individual might accompany the instructor to an actual business, watch him complete an application, and watch a videotaped interview.

Role Playing – A chance is given to practice the skill in a pretend situation. The instructor can act as a potential employer and conduct a mock application and interview process.

Behavior Rehearsal – The skill is practiced in a real situation with the instructor. The instructor might arrange for the individual to apply at a business sensitive to the individual's unique situation.

In-vivo Practice – The skill is practiced in real life situations, alone, and repeatedly if possible. The instructor might have the individual apply for a job at two businesses each week.

Behaviorism

Behaviorism is based on the idea of encouraging or discouraging certain behaviors using reinforcement through reward or punishment. Behaviorism is commonly used in a variety of educational approaches and environments. Behavior in the form of progress toward achieving a skill can be reinforced with positive or negative rewards. Behavior in the form of inadequate progress can be reinforced with positive or negative punishment. Positive refers to something that is added while negative is something removed. Punishment should be used cautiously as it can cause resentment and damage a relationship with a client. Rewards have greater potential, especially if used carefully so as to be meaningful and communicate to the client his progress. A number of people have objected to this approach to education in any area including skills training as being too insensitive and lacking human compassion.

Skills Generalization and Maintenance

Skills generalization refers to the ability to apply a skill learned in a specific situation to other situations. This is a common problem for PsyR professionals. Individuals who are successful in a controlled instructional environment or even a limited real life environment often have problems applying the skill elsewhere. Research has shown that this is a common problem for many people, not just those with mental illness. Skills maintenance is the ability to stay proficient at a skill over time. This should always be a concern for PsyR professionals, especially if clients will not be continually practice the skill. PsyR professionals should take care to help clients maintain existing skills, learn new skills, and maintain new skills. Paying close attention to the maintenance of existing skills gives clients confidence by highlighting their strengths. This confidence is crucial in the process of learning new things.

Recovery

Traditional concepts of recovery focus on a complete cure or return to normal functioning. With most major mental illness, this traditional concept does not occur since these illnesses usually last a lifetime. Psychiatric rehabilitation professions can offer the hope of recovery to individuals with an alternate definition. This definition includes a several step process that does not always follow a certain order. One step is acceptance of the illness. This includes changing one's goals and life expectations to fit this acceptance. Another step is the understanding that temporary setbacks, failure, and even relapse will occur. Building a new and acceptable self image and positive outlook is another key step. Recovery is more likely to occur with mental health professionals recognize that each person will have a very unique path to recovery and work under that belief.

Important Terms

Impairment: Lack of normal function from a physical, biological, or psychological perspective such as experiencing delusions or inability to sleep.

Dysfunction: Not being able to complete a chore or job or participate in an activity that most people could, or not to the same level or in the same way as most people, such as not being able to maintain personal hygiene or communicate with co-workers.

Disability: Not being able complete to requirements of a specific job or role that most people could such as providing shelter for oneself or holding a job.

Disadvantage: Being without certain opportunities to such as extent one cannot complete certain tasks or be part of certain activities that most people of similar age, gender, or culture could such as experiencing racial discrimination or lack of education.

Psychodynamic: Theory that asserts that mental illness is a result of unresolved problems buried deep in an individual's mind.

Psychoanalytic: An approach popularized by Freud that emphasizes exploring the inner mind and looking carefully at the past.

Diathesis-stress model: A theory that suggests that some people who are already biologically susceptible to mental illnesses can become symptomatic because of certain stresses.

Delphi technique: A research approach that acquires information by questioning experts in that area or field.

Eugenics: A scientific field that focuses on changing or refining hereditary characteristics in a specific species, breed, or race.

Longitudinal study: Research approach that follows participants and documents results over an extended period of time, usually ten years or longer.

Treatment: Emphasizes reducing unwanted symptoms with the goal of improving an individual's overall state of well-being.

Crisis intervention: Emphasizes management and correction of situations that pose an immediate threat to an individual and/or others in order to insure safety.

Case management: Focuses on helping an individual access resources and get desired or necessary services from a variety of community, government, and private sources.

Rehabilitation: Seeks to understand an individual's goals and desires and help them get the skills and assistance needed to reach those goals.

Enrichment: Emphasizes getting an individual involved in enjoyable activities and programs that allow him a chance to grow personally.

Rights protection: Seeks to help an individual have equal opportunities under the law and within society by looking out for his rights.

Basic support: Focuses on ensuring an individual has the basic necessities of live such as housing, food, and medical care.

Self-help: Emphasizes the importance of personal choice and involvement in all decisions affecting one's life.

Wellness: Works with an individual to provide guidance in living healthy such as nutrition, exercise, medication maintenance, and lifestyle changes.

Education and Employment

Obstacles to Employment

The stigma of mental illness is perpetuated by many media sources created the belief that individuals with mental illness are always unstable or dangerous. These individuals themselves tend to absorb these messages from society, increasing self-doubt and decreasing confidence. Misguided services provided by professionals lacking information are also a problem. Underestimating the abilities of or not recognized the needs of clients can dramatically reduce their chances at meaningful, long-term employment. Limited vocation experience or training due to chronic illness, keeps many individuals from finding. The actual mental illness a person has can itself create disabilities that make employment difficult to get. This includes symptoms, cycles of the disease, medication side effects, and limited activities. Many individuals with serious mental illness seek government benefits. These can be lost or reduced if the individual finds employment. This can be scary for those individuals who fear a relapse with no security to fall back on.

Effective Vocational Programs

- Client choice – Allow individuals to pick the services that match up with their needs and goals.
- Integrated environment – Services, support, and real-life situations should interact.
- Service connection – Services are easy to access for all areas of life, not just job related.
- Natural supports – Training individuals to use services and support systems that exist in their normal environment.
- Quick placement – Individuals are moved from training to actual jobs as fast as possible with support in place.
- Job accommodation – Once employed, individuals receive job modifications that help them be successful and comply with the law.
- Uninterrupted services – Individuals get help in all needed areas and professionals providing the services remain constant.
- Employer education – Employer needs and concerns are recognized and employers are educated about the valuable contributions individuals with mental illness make and encouraged not to view hiring as philanthropy.
- Supported employment – Environment for workers with disabilities in which they receive full time on the job support in their work environment. In the enclave or work crew model, a small group of individuals with disabilities works for the same business or employer. This group is no larger than eight in size and often works in a contained unit. However, it is possible for members of the enclave to work in different areas of the business. A job coach stays with the group during the entire shift and provides training, assistance, and support. This type of work environment is covered by the Federal Rehabilitation Act. This type of program has the disadvantages of still isolated those with disabilities such as mental illness from other workers and also limits individual choice in the type of job.

Perception Changes

The stigma of mental illness prevents many individuals from pursuing goals including higher education. Uninformed misconceptions lead many staff and administrators at institutions of higher learning to expect violent, disruptive behavior or a lack of academic performance. Even mental health professionals sometimes underestimate the abilities of individuals with mental illness and fail to provide support for educational goals. A person's actual mental illness can pose a disability that interferes with the requirements of postsecondary education. Anxiety, stress, and difficulty concentrating are problematic. Also, the individual may have gaps in basic skills from previous interrupted learning due to the illness. The cost and coordination of pursing postsecondary education may also seem overwhelming. Financial aid, registration, applying, scheduling classes, and getting transportation are all examples.

- Completed and ongoing studies about the course and possible outcomes of schizophrenia
- New and improved medications for treating mental illness that are more effective in managing positive and negative symptoms, and have fewer undesirable side effects
- Documented positive outcomes in the areas of employment, life skills, housing, and relationships for individuals receiving psychiatric rehabilitation services as well as continued improvements in this field based on research
- Better education and information availability which as improved community understanding about mental illness, reducing stigma, overturning many myths and misconceptions about schizophrenia and other mental illness, and increasing acceptance of mental illness

When drug treatments were first developed for individuals with mental illness over fifty years ago, many people, including mental health professionals, believed the problems was solved and rehabilitation would not be needed to return people successfully to the community. The reality is that while powerful in reducing symptoms and hospitalization time, psychiatric drugs are only part of the complete picture. Rehabilitation must exist along with treatment so that individuals can get the skills and support needed to function within the community. Even the most recently developed medications still only improve a person's willingness to be part of the rehabilitation process. Drugs cannot teach skills needed for employment, help individuals find housing, or improve someone's social life. An accurate view of psychiatric medications recognizes that it is an appropriate intervention used in combination with rehabilitation.

Influence on Research

Individuals with mental illness have increasing opportunities to influence the research being conducted to help them. The federal government has issued mandates requiring the use of Participatory Action Research (PAR) which is an approach that includes individuals in the research planning, development, implementation, and analysis, who are part of the group being studied. This allows individuals with mental illness to take leadership positions that can guide research in a way that is most beneficial to themselves and others. It also allows individuals with mental illness to define the outcomes that research should be measuring. Recent examples of this approach have identified empowerment, satisfaction, well-being, and ability to help oneself as important measures. Psychiatric rehabilitation practitioners continue to advocate for increased involvement of their client in all aspects of the PsyR movement.

The ADA

Since individuals with mental illness qualify as disabled under this federal legislation, they qualify for the protections the law provides. According to the ADA, employers cannot discriminate against someone in the employment process due to a disability. This includes all areas of employment such as hiring, termination, promotion, and benefits. The ADA requires employers to consider all qualified applicants for a job, regardless of disabilities, even if job accommodations will be required, as long as the person can perform the required aspects of the job. The law requires employers to make necessary accommodations for an employee as long as they are reasonable in cost and application. Also, in the hiring process, employees cannot question an applicant about any obvious or possible disability. Employers with fewer than fifteen employees are exempt from this legislation.

Workplace Accommodations

Assistance from others –This can include a job coach or mentor, extra training, and support from colleagues.

Policy changes – This is the most common area of accommodation and can include many different options. For someone with trouble concentrating, a quiet work area can be arranged or telecommuting might be offered. To accommodate illness related absences, telecommuting might be offered, sick leave might be taken in advance, job sharing might be available, alternate schedules can be allowed, and temporary workers hired for long absences.

Management or supervisors – The employee's supervisors and company managers could be provided with extra training in the individual's unique needs, management strategies for workers with disabilities, and guidelines for complying with ADA.

Co-workers – Training can be provided to co-workers of an employee with mental illness to encourage respect, acceptance, and integration into the workplace community. This can include education about mental illness to discourage rumors, myths, and the spread of misinformation.

Transitional Employment (TE)

This type of program allows individuals to experience one or more temporary jobs in preparation for future permanent work. The organization or agency sponsoring the program arranges for control over a job with an employer. They promise to keep the job filled at all times. Staff members learn the job and then train clients to do it. Clients hold the job for a designated period, often several months, before they move on and another client moves in. During this time, the agency or organization provides support for the client. In transitional employment programs, clients ideally have a chance to try a number of jobs. Jobs in this type of program are usually part time and require little or no skills. This allows access to the largest number of clients possible.

Role of a Job Coach

Job coaches are also known as employment specialists and employment or human resource consultants. Their primary purpose is to assist individuals with disabilities obtain meaningful employment. This requires them to be knowledgeable in the areas of career planning, marketing, and networking within different industries, as well in all areas of working with people who have mental illnesses. A job coach often starts with a detailed assessment of a client's skills, strengths, interests, level of required support, and any other areas relevant to securing employment. Other aspects of this job include training, on-the-job support, training employers, money management assistance, facilitating transportation, helping clients build relationships with co-workers, and understanding benefits. Job coaches also educated clients about all other available resources including family members, government agencies, and community organizations.

Supported Employment

Supported employment (SE) is an environment for workers with disabilities in which they receive full time on the job support in their work environment. In the enclave or work crew model, a small group of individuals with disabilities works for the same business or employer. This group is no larger than eight in size and often works in a contained unit. However, it is possible for members of the enclave to work in different areas of the business. A job coach stays with the group during the entire shift and provides training, assistance, and support. This type of work environment is covered by the Federal Rehabilitation Act. This type of program has the disadvantages of still isolated those with disabilities such as mental illness from other workers and also limits individual choice in the type of job.

The characteristics that supported employment must have in order to be effective:

- The client must be an active participant in the job search process and his values, interests, and preferences must be a driving force in job selection
- Enough time must be allowed for the client to select a job without undue pressure
- Extensive selections of jobs and job categories are necessary for clients to find one for which they are best suited
- Places of employment must offer growth, promotion, and career opportunities instead of transitional and basic level jobs
- All workplace members need adequate training and knowledge about mental illness so that the client is not ostracized or alienated and can be productive
- Support should be available at the place of employment and outside of work if needed

IPE

An important step in the vocational rehabilitation process is the design of an IPE (Individual Plan for Employment) that is unique to the person being served. This plan is created with the joint effort of the client and rehabilitation counselor. Services that might be provided during this stage include skills training; job coaching, transportation, education advancement, referral services, advocacy, and job placement. The IPE is the foundation of an individual's plan for obtaining meaningful employment and should be considered a significant step and given serious thought. This plan is developed by considered client goals, interests, skills, and needed supports. The plan details needed services that will be provided or for which resources must be accessed.

Stakeholders in the IPE system are:

- Psychiatrists and psychologists
- Counselors in private and public practice
- Marriage and family therapists
- Hospitals, residential treatment facilities, and outpatient clinics
- Day centers
- Clubhouses or member programs
- Supported housing programs
- Supported educational programs

- Supported employment programs
- Vocational training programs
- Psychiatric rehabilitation practitioners
- Social workers
- Public health officials on the local, county, state, and national level
- Individuals with mental illness
- Family members of individuals with mental illness
- Self-help groups for individuals with mental illness
- Local law enforcement officials
- Government entitlement programs such as SSI, SSDI, HUD, and EEOC

Employment Resources

Job club – This is an organization focused on providing its members with all the tools and resources needed to seek employment. This includes training in needed skills such as interviewing and completing applications, access to equipment and technology such as phones and computers, and a peer support network.

Sheltered workshops – This is a group or agency that obtains specific manufacturing jobs from area business. These jobs are completed by individuals with disabilities in a supervised environment. Employees are paid for each item they complete based on the production rate of non-disabled workers. This resource can be an initial step to finding a job in a competitive marketplace or a permanent job for those with severe disabilities.

Affirmative industries – These are businesses owned by an agency assisting people with disabilities. The agency employs its clients to work in these businesses. Contracts are obtained with area businesses and individuals for the services the agency business can provide. Clients working in this environment have good work experience with needed support, but have few choices in their job.

Employment Opportunities

Touring businesses in the community and seeing different jobs that exist can expand knowledge about employment possibilities. Volunteering is an option that can build confidence and skills in a lower pressure environment than a paying job. It also provides exposure to a wide variety of work environments. Job sampling programs are sometimes available with local employers offering individuals a few hours of work to help them consider opportunities. These programs are often unpaid although government rehabilitation agencies might pay individuals. Job shadowing allows and individual to follow another person to his job and observe for a period of time to get a better understanding of the nature and requirements of that line of work. Informational interviews can also provide insight by giving individuals a chance to ask questions of people in different fields. A new type of program of interest is the interactive internship which combines detailed assessment of an individual's interests, abilities, and skills and matches that person with a particular field or occupation. An internship is arranged that might be paying or not, depending on the situation. These programs are encouraged for people with a true interest in pursuing a career path, not just finding a job.

Important Terms

Client choice: Allow individuals to pick the services that match up with their needs and goals.

Integrated environment: Services, support, and real-life situations should interact.

Service connection: Services are easy to access for all areas of life, not just job related.

Natural supports: Training individuals to use services and support systems that exist in their normal environment.

Quick placement: Individuals are moved from training to actual jobs as fast as possible with support in place.

Job accommodation: Once employed, individuals receive job modifications that help them be successful and comply with the law.

Uninterrupted services: Individuals get help in all needed areas and professionals providing the services remain constant.

Employer education: Employer needs and concerns are recognized and employers are educated about the valuable contributions individuals with mental illness make and encouraged not to view hiring as philanthropy.

Housing Options

Boarding Houses and SROs

Advantages

- Low cost
- Competent operators can provide transportation for residents to day programs, treatment appointments, and jobs
- Can provide a supportive, home-like atmosphere
- Can provide a transitional environment for moving from residential treatment or hospitalization towards independent living

Disadvantages

- Potential for abuse by unscrupulous operators
- Commonly located in unsafe, inner-city areas
- Does not offer the most normalized environment
- Can promote behaviors associated with institutionalization such as isolation, avoiding others, unemployment, and poor social interaction
- Residents often lack privacy

Fairweather Lodges

Advantages

- Extensive support provided by on-site professional staff gradually transitioning to more independent living
- Lodges operate businesses that offer employment and even ownership opportunities for residents
- More positive option than hospitalization for those with severe illness
- Promotes cooperative problem solving skills
- Some lodges allow members to live and work outside the lodge, but still partake of support

Disadvantages

- Does not offer the most normalized environment, interaction with larger community is limited
- Stigma can be attached to living in a group home
- Socialization limited mainly to others with mental illness
- Employment options are limited

Residential Treatment Facilities

Advantages

- Operated by trained mental health professionals
- Support and care are available 24 hours a day
- Environment totally focused on improving an individual's well being and ability to function
- Medication can be monitored

- Some programs are flexible and allow time away from facility for work, school, or overnight stays
- Environment is usually more nurturing and home-like than hospitals and institutions
- Support is provided in daily living skills such as cooking, grooming, and cleaning

Disadvantages

- Sometimes rehabilitation services are limited
- Environment is not normalized
- Interaction with the larger community can be limited
- Stigma is often attached in the form of community misunderstanding and fear of residents, neighborhood opposition to the home, threatened lawsuits, and community isolation

Linear Continuum Model

This an approach that emphasizes the transition from institutional to independent living as a multi-step process based on the following concepts. First, a program should utilize a variety of housing options that vary in the amount of support provided as well as the level of restriction. Second, the program should require clients to move from the level with the highest support and restrictions to the level with the least. This process should be efficient, but tailored to individual needs. Next, at each level, the clients currently participating should have achieved similar function and progress. Finally, the end goal is to achieve independent living status outside of the program. During this process, a client who has a setback requiring hospitalization will start again at the lowest level. These types of programs are typically available to a small number of clients and have limited research to back up their long-term effectiveness. Some aspects that have been documented with negative results are the constant state of impending change or instability, lack of skills training on site at each level, and limits on choice and privacy.

Supported Housing Approach

The supported housing approach emphasizes the importance of individual choice in house options, made successful by providing the level and type of support each unique person needs. This model considers all housing options available, and works with clients to accommodate their desired housing. This approach also values specific environments that respect individual choice, limiting rules, schedules, and structure that apply to everyone. Self-determination is the key element of this approach, supported mental health professionals in areas such as locating housing, landlord relations, financial management, independent living skills, financial assistance and entitlements, and resolving conflicts. This approach has been successful enough to convince some states to redirect funds for psychiatric hospitals into independent housing. Initial research into this approach has indicated increased housing stability and fewer incidents of hospitalization as well as clients' reports of greater quality of life, more hope, and greater happiness with their lives.

Rehabilitation Centers

Early psychosocial rehabilitation centers, like Fountain House, were created by individuals with mental illness who often described themselves as "ex-patients". The centers were intended to provide a social forum for these individuals to help and support one another as well as others with mental illness. Modern centers like Fellowship House in Miami and Portals House in Los Angeles, embrace the psychiatric rehabilitation approach on a comprehensive level. From the earliest centers to the well-respected today, a common goal has been the individual development of skills and strategies for coping with mental illness. The level of success achieved by psychosocial rehabilitation centers supports the idea that support and assistance should be provided in a person's chosen environment and that peer involvement can be valuable.

Independent Living Movement

The independent living movement has grown through concerted efforts by individuals with disabilities to increase their ability to live independently and become advocates for their own rights. These individuals, facing similar concerns and challenges, have started to work together to demand equal opportunities in all areas of life, including housing. This movement is based on the belief that it is external obstacles such as physical impediments and people's attitudes that prevent independent living, not disabilities. The movement also emphasizes the importance of individual choice, even the right to make risky or ill-advised decisions. The prevailing belief in this movement is that most disabled individuals can take care of themselves with training and support. This movement has led to the creation of independent living centers or resource organizations for individuals with disabilities, operated by individuals with disabilities. These centers provide training, socialization, peer support, personal assistance services, and more, all provided by staff hired by the clients themselves.

Housing Laws

Fair Housing Act

This law was originally passed in 1968 and has been amended several times since. It is enforced by the Department of Housing and Urban Development (HUD). The law prohibits discrimination against individuals with disabilities, including mental illness, in many housing related areas. Individuals cannot refuse to sell to, rent to, or provide financing for individuals based on their disability. Different requirements for selling or renting conditions based on the disability are also prohibited.

Section 504 of the Rehabilitation Act

This law was passed in 1973 and prohibits discrimination on the basis of disability by any program receiving federal financial assistance. In the area of housing, this could include government subsidized or guaranteed loans or public housing assistance.

Title II of the Americans with Disabilities Act

This law was passed in 1990 and prohibits discrimination based on disability, including mental illness in all services or programs receiving federal funding. HUD enforces this in regards to housing programs, public housing, and housing referrals.

Section 8 Vouchers

Section 8 vouchers and certificates are basically a government subsidy to offset the cost of housing for individuals who meet certain income qualifications. One of the goals of this program is to provide low income individuals with more choice in housing markets while avoided concentration of such individuals in any one housing complex. The old Section 8 program has been combined with the newer Housing Choice Voucher Program Recipients of this entitlement pay no more than 40% of their income to the landlord of their choice. The local PHA provides payment to the landlord for the remaining amount based on market value as determined by HUD. The local PHA has the ability to determine preferential placement of certain categories of individuals, including those with disabilities, based on local conditions. Waiting lists for this program are often lengthy and application periods very brief.

Help from PHA

PHA's (Planned Housing Agencies) are officially regulated by HUD although recent trends have given greater control to local authorities in the management of housing resources. PHA's oversee a number of federal housing programs including Section 8 vouchers and subsidies and federal public housing. PHA's are directed by an elected or appointed local commission or board which reconciles local need with federal government policies and guidelines. Federal public housing is owned and operated by local PHA's. Rent from tenants cannot exceed fixed percentages of income, usually 30% or less and HUD provides the funds to cover all expenses not collected in rent. Due to the high level of local control, PHA's can establish preferential tenant categories including limits on public housing for individuals with disabilities.

Community Development Block Grant

The Community Development Block Grant is designed to provide housing options, improve the quality of living, and increase economic opportunity for individuals in low and moderate income brackets. Communities receiving this funding must dedicate at least 70% percent of their funds to this purpose. Municipalities or groups of municipal entities that apply for this funding can use it for housing rehabilitation loans, non-profit home construction such as Habitat for Humanity, purchasing land or buildings, building shelters for homeless individuals, neighborhood or community centers, relocating displaced individuals, improving accessibility for individuals with disabilities, and providing employment services and even child care to assist individuals in obtaining jobs or job training.

SHP

The SHP (Supportive Housing Program) is primarily designed to assist homeless people in finding housing and receiving necessary support services. This program provides assistance is securing temporary housing to transition individuals off the streets and to provide supportive housing environments to ease individuals into more independent and eventual permanent living situations. Supportive services include financial training, independent living skills, and negotiating with landlords and sellers. Funds are used to assist individuals through purchases, rentals, and temporary shelter. Homeless individuals diagnosed with disabilities, including mental illness, can qualify for additional supportive services. This program supports Safe Haven services which offer highly supported living environments, often with communal kitchen and/or bath facilities, and basic needs such as clothing and food. These programs provide a first step into more permanent living situations.

The Shelter Plus Care Program

The Shelter Plus Care Program is intended to help homeless individuals with disabilities find permanent shelter through special rental programs with private individuals or organizations. The individuals served by this program frequently have mental illnesses and/or substance abuse problems. Government agencies and locally controlled Planned Housing Agencies can apply for this money. The funds can be used to support several different types of rental programs including tenant based rental programs which award grants for the assistance of individuals living in housing options of their choice. Other programs are sponsor based rentals, which usually involve administration by a non-profit group or government agency which applied for the grant, or the project based programs or single residence occupancy dwellings run by private individuals or groups who agree to use funds to complete a certain amount of building rehabilitation.

Regulations

HIPAA

- Individuals can ask to view and receive copies of all their medical records
- Individuals must be notified of legal ways their health records can be used or shared with others
- Individuals can have inaccuracies or omissions fixed on their health records
- Individuals get to decide if their health information can be used or shared under certain circumstances such as for marketing research
- Individuals have the right to a report that documents when and why personal health information was shared
- Individuals have the right to a grievance process if they believe their rights or medical privacy have been violated by going through their medical provider or the US government

Under HIPAA, personal medical information may be shared:

- For coordinating the care and treatment of an individual
- To facilitate insurance or third-party payment to doctors, hospitals, and other service providers
- Family members or other people the individual designates
- To governing and regulatory agencies overseeing conditions and practices of medical service providers
- To protect the general public by providing knowledge about potentially epidemic illnesses such as the flu and certain sexually transmitted diseases
- To comply with local, state, or federal regulations regarding required reporting to police as in cases of domestic abuse or gunshot wounds

Under HIPAA, personal medical information may NOT be shared without an individual's consent:

- With his or her employer
- For advertising or marketing purposes
- Includes notes or dictation from counseling sessions

Services of Individual States

While each state individually administers Medicaid and has some discretion in determining recipients, the federal government has identified the following groups that states must provide services for:

- Families who meet the eligibility requirements for the Aid to Dependent Families and Children program
- Pregnant women and children younger than 6 whose family income is 133% of the federally determined poverty level
- Children ages 6-19 whose family income is at the federally determined poverty level

- Children up to age 18, or 19 if still in school, cared for by legal guardians other than their parents
- Individuals with disabilities that qualify them to receive Supplemental Security Income (SSI) payments.

Medicare Part B

Medicare Part B covers visits to the following mental health professionals providing the professional accepts Medicare payments:

- Doctors
- Nurse practitioners and physician's assistants
- Clinical social workers
- Clinical psychologists

Medicare Part B covers the following types of services:

- Individual, group, and occupational therapy by state licensed providers
- Lab tests
- Administration of medication that cannot be self-administered
- Family counseling
- Client education regarding the mental illness
- Testing or assessment to determine appropriateness and effectiveness of current treatment plan
- Partial hospitalization if your doctor states that the only other alternative is in-patient treatment

Medicare Part B *excludes* the following from coverage:

- Meals at and transportation to and from mental health care providers
- Support groups outside an approved practitioners office
- Prescriptions that can be self-administered
- Job or skills training

Medicare Part A

Medicare Part A covers the following:

- In-patient treatment in a specialty psychiatric facility that accepts Medicare for up to 190 days during the individual's lifetime
- In-patient treatment in a general hospital that accepts Medicare with no lifetime limit
- Hospital costs minus preset individual deductible and per day costs for up to 150 days each benefit period

Individuals covered by Medicare Part A are expected to pay the following:

- Deductible each benefit period of hospitalization of $912that covers a stay of up to 60 days
- $228 each day of a stay for days 61-90
- $456 each day of a stay for days 90-150
- All hospitalization costs for a stay for days 151+

Medicare Part A *excludes* the following:

- Private duty nursing
- A private room unless determined to be medically necessary by the treating physician
- Telephone or television access
- All hospital costs if the stay exceeds 150 days

Medicare Terms

Assignment: When a doctor or other provider agrees the accept and agreed upon amount from Medicare as full payment for services.

Benefit period: Measurement used by Medicare to govern hospital stays, beginning the day an individual enters the facility; a new period starts if the individual has gone 60 days without hospitalization or skilled nursing.

Lifetime reserve days: Period of 60 days that can be used once in an individual's lifetime if hospitalization goes past 150 days; daily coinsurance applies.

Medicare Part A: Coverage for hospitalization.

Medicare Part B: Coverage for services from a doctor, therapist, or other medical provider.

Active treatment: Treatment plan individualized for resolving or addressing a condition.

Systems Competencies

Fighting Mental Illness Stigmas

Much of the stigma attached to mental illness comes from ignorance. Mental health professionals have an obligation of work to educate the general population about the reality of mental illness. This includes advocating the latest in technology to improve diagnoses and understanding, supporting research and development of new medications, and providing interaction opportunities for people to relate to those with mental illness. Mental health professionals should encourage the integration of mentally ill clients into general society whenever possible, instead of overusing institutions. Mental health professionals should advocate for all opportunities possible for their clients to experience full and normal lives among others without mental illness.

Supported Education (SEd)

Self-Contained Classroom

In this type of program, all students have some type of psychiatric disability. They attend classes together, following a set curriculum which usually emphasizes career planning and teaching skills with extensive support provided. The classroom is physically on the campus of the school sponsoring the program so individuals can use school resources and participate in other activities. These programs are a preparatory step for higher education or finding a job. This type of environment is the least normalized and provides limited interaction with people without mental illness.

On-Site Model

This type of program focuses on helping individuals with psychiatric disabilities find and use the resources that are already available at an institution of higher learning. This can include programs such as tutoring, counseling, and peer support.

Mobile Support Model

This type of program utilizes professional support staff that travel to help individuals with mental illness reach educational goals. This includes providing help on and off campus and is very individualized to each student.

Elements of a Comprehensive System

Treatment – emphasizes reducing unwanted symptoms with the goal of improving an individual's overall state of well-being

Crisis intervention – emphasizes management and correction of situations that pose an immediate threat to an individual and/or others in order to insure safety

Case management – focuses on helping an individual access resources and get desired or necessary services from a variety of community, government, and private sources

Rehabilitation – seeks to understand an individual's goals and desires and help them get the skills and assistance needed to reach those goals

Enrichment – emphasizes getting an individual involved in enjoyable activities and programs that allow him a chance to grow personally

Rights protection – seeks to help an individual have equal opportunities under the law and within society by looking out for his rights

Basic support – focuses on ensuring an individual has the basic necessities of live such as housing, food, and medical care

Self-help – emphasizes the importance of personal choice and involvement in all decisions affecting one's life

Wellness – works with an individual to provide guidance in living healthy such as nutrition, exercise, medication maintenance, and lifestyle changes

SSI Program

Unlike SSDI, the SSI program does not require a history of Social Security contributions for eligibility. Eligibility is determined by meeting the Social Security definition of disability and demonstrating specific financial need. Disability is defined as a medical condition or other impairment that prevents substantial gainful employment (SGA) for a period of at least one year. This includes inability to work in fields of previous experience or any other available work options. SGA is currently defined as earning less than $860 each month. Additionally, there must be evidence that the disability is expected to last longer than a year. Currently financial need is determined by liquid assets less than $2000 or $3000 for a couple and monthly income less than $856 or $1492 for a couple. Program benefits are available immediately upon determination of eligibility and in some cases can even start while the case is being reviewed, known as presumptive eligibility.

CCS and CSP

The CSS (Community Support System) idea and the CSP (Community Support Programs) grew out of the work of NIMH in the 1970's as a plan to provide and connect all the services and resources in the community that an individual with mental illness would need to access. Initial and ongoing research was used to determine which areas should be emphasized. These identified services and resources included identifying individuals in need of services and contacting them, treatment for mental illness, general medical care, self-help or peer groups, employment, government benefits, crisis intervention, housing, protection of rights and representation, and support from family and others. Case management is often a component in order to facilitate access to all services and resources. CSP is funded with federal money at the state and local level.

Supported Environments

- The supported environment is not part of the recognized mental health establishment but rather more normalized places such as an apartment, a college classroom, or an office
- An individual is allowed to be part of the environment without receiving mental health services such as enrolling in a class or renting an apartment
- The environment is based on individual choice, not mental health service requirements
- The environment should afford individuals many choices not tied to any particular plan or progressive program, just as real life offers those choices
- Within the environment, individuals are free to choose the level and type of support they want, when they want support, or to choose no support at all.

SSDI

SSDI (Social Security Disability Insurance) is a program funded by taxpayer contributions into Social Security, offering benefits to individuals who have contributed to FICA for 40 quarters which equates to 10 years. Benefits can also be available for the individual's spouse or child. The individual must meet the SSA's definition of disability which is a medical condition or other impairment that prevents substantial gainful employment (SGA) for a period of at least one year. This includes inability to work in fields of previous experience or any other available work options. SGA is currently defined as earning less than $860 each month. Benefits can begin five months after disability is established and monthly payments will be calculated using a formula tied to the individual's earnings history. Payments are made one month behind. Benefits will continue as long as the disability is present and periodic review will be conducted to determine eligibility. At age 65, benefits stop as Social Security benefits begin.

IDEA

The protection provided for individuals with disabilities by the Individuals With Disabilities Act (IDEA) protects the rights of children with disabilities, including mental illness, to receive a free, appropriate public education. This program requires public schools to create and Individualized Education Program (IEP) for children meeting this definition. The IEP will detail all services and programs that will be provided to the child in order to meet his unique needs. The IEP must also be implemented in the least restrictive and most normalized educational environment possible. IEPs are developed by qualified professional personnel but require the involvement of teachers, parents, and in some cases, the child. At least once a year, the IEP must be reconsidered and appropriate changes made. Complaints about these procedures can be directed to the US Department of Education.

Alternate Provider Programs

Alternate Provider and Ticket to Work Programs are both designed to encourage the provision of services to disabled individuals, including those with mental illness, with the end goal of ending the receipt of government entitlements by those individuals. With the Alternate Provider Program, public or private agencies or organizations can receive a one time payment equal to a portion of the individual's annual government entitlements after all receipt of those payments has ended due to the individual finding sufficient employment. The Ticket to Work Program operates under the same basic idea. The main difference is that the service provider, often referred to as and Employment Network (EN), and receives partial payments at several steps along the process instead of only at the end. Additionally, payments continue to be made to the service provider for up to five additional years, encouraging long-term support of independence and freedom from need of government entitlements. If an individual begins receiving entitlements again during that period, the EN no longer receives payments.

Projects with Industry

Projects with Industry (PWI) are one program funded by Title VI with the goal of helping more individuals with disabilities to find employment. The program seeks to build relationships between government agencies and local industries and businesses to accomplish this goal. The program can provide on the job training, funding for resources, job placement services, and skills training. Grants, for these programs, last five years once they are awarded. Title VI also funds Supported Employment (SE) services which help individuals with the most severe disabilities find and keep jobs through job coaches, job sharing, special technology, and transportation assistance. Employers are encouraged to participate with benefits that include fully screened employees, employee matching services, and full time and ongoing support from professional job coaches.

ADA Title II

Title II of the ADA specifically applies to all local and state government regardless of size of acceptance of funds from the federal government. Title II mandates that government entities provide equal access to all programs and services. This includes such areas as benefits of parks, libraries, and recreation programs. It also includes opportunities for government employment as well as use of public health facilities, government buildings, the justice system, and voting. Public transportation such as city buses and subway systems are also covered. Although government agencies and organizations must make all reasonable efforts to provide services and programs that do not discriminated based on disability, they are not required to make changes that are financially excessive or change the basic nature of the service or program in question. The US Department of Justice handles most complaints of violations of this law. Any complaint or grievance must be filed within 180 days of the actual violation of this law. Transportation related complaints are handled by the US Department of Transportation, Civil Rights Violations division.

SAMHSA

SAMHSA's main goal or mission is to provide the opportunity for all individuals to live within the community regardless of mental illness or substance abuse problems. The following are sub-goals designed to achieve the overall mission:

- Change our country's mental health system
- Increase the number of individuals that our mental health system can treat
- Increase the choices of individuals with mental illness or substance abuse problems
- Obtain better life quality and treatment results for people with dual diagnosis of mental illness and substance abuse problem
- Use sound scientific and research-based knowledge to improve services to clients
- Lessen substance abuse among teenagers by limiting access
- Provide better services related to disaster

Tools used by SAMHSA to achieve its goals include:

- Grants to community agencies and organizations
- Funding research and clinical studies
- Providing information and training to mental health providers and the entire community
- Coordinating numerous programs whose services can benefit those with mental illness or substance abuse problems

Tools of SAMHSA

- Access to a social network of individuals with common experiences to form new relationships and overcome stigma and isolation
- Assistance in moving from helplessness and dependence to self-reliance and increased self-confidence
- Learning new coping strategies based on the failures and successes of others
- Escape from the constant structure and rigor of treatment in an environment of self-determination

- Improved interaction and productivity in society through increased confidence and effective coping skills
- The opportunity to function as a role-model for others by sharing experiences and wisdom
- Availability of a support network for times of crisis or relapse

Subgroups Rehabilitation

Psychiatric rehabilitation is for those people who have a major mental illness which interferes in some way with their life functions. Psychiatric rehabilitation practitioners should consider each person individually, but also as a member of one or more of the following subgroups:

- Specific age groups such as senior citizens or teenagers
- Economically disadvantaged
- Homeless
- Members of identified minority groups such as by race or ethnicity
- Dual diagnosis of severe mental illness and physical disability
- Dual diagnosis of severe mental illness and substance abuse problems
- Dual diagnosis of severe mental illness and developmental disabilities

Treatment Versus Rehabilitation

The goal of psychiatric treatment is to cure an individual's disease or at least reduce the undesired symptoms. This is accomplished primarily through evaluating symptoms and determining the history of the individual's illness. Treatment is then designed from a variety of options including psychotherapy, group therapy, medications, and behavior modifications. The goal of psychiatric rehabilitation is to help an individual operate in his chosen situation with maximum functioning and fulfillment. This is accomplished by determining the individual's specific needs and desires, skills, and available resources. Practitioners focus on helping the individual learn needed skills, discover and access resources, and alter his environment to reach his goals. While psychiatric treatment emphasizes traditional theories and medial approaches as a broad approach to mental illness, psychiatric rehabilitation if very focused on individual needs and goals.

Moral Therapy Era

The moral therapy era is a period during the 1800's of improving care for clients with mental illness. One of the treatment approaches used then was conducting a complete analysis of the impact of the person's illness on all aspects of his life such as at his job, in recreation activities, and in social interactions as part of treatment. This idea has carried into the modern psychiatric approach of completely assessing how a person functions in the community. Additionally, during the moral therapy era it was seen that specific engaging activities can help individuals as much or even more than traditional therapy alone. This idea is a cornerstone of psychiatric rehabilitation with its focus on engaging individuals in activities to improve their lives such as training, job searches, interaction with support groups, and learning life skills.

CMHC

The Vocational Rehabilitation Act of 1943 first opened up access to financial aid and eligibility for vocational programs to individuals with severe mental illnesses. Many state vocational programs provided desperately needed skill training to disabled individuals, who were now defined to include major mental illness. Vocational training, skills acquisition, and employment assistance have become key components of psychiatric rehabilitation and state vocational programs often meet this need. Community mental health centers (CMHC) although they were a failure in successfully meeting the comprehensive needs of individuals with mental illness were one of the first groups to introduce the idea of providing support, treatment, and crisis intervention to individuals in their chosen environment. This is a key aspect of psychiatric rehabilitation today.

One physical technique for stress reduction is Progressive Muscular Relaxation (PMR). PMR teaches a person to contract a set of muscles as tightly as possible and hold it for several seconds. The person should let the muscles go back to inactive and then focus on relaxing the muscles as much as possible. This technique can be used with one muscle group or the entire body. Another physical technique is simple, controlled breathing in which the person focuses on taking a specific number of deep breaths and slow releases. Biofeedback is another technique helpful in reducing stress by promoting relaxation. Biofeedback uses electronic sensors to measure physical reactions such as skin temperature, heart rate, and muscle movement while individuals engage in specific activities including experimenting with stress reduction. This gives immediate insight into the effect of specific techniques and actions.

Conceptual Model of Recovery

The conceptual model of recovery is based on the following four elements:

- Hope – This element is based on a person's belief that recovery can happen. It starts with acceptance of a problem and a willingness to seek change. It is built around recognizing and exploiting strengths. It encourages an attitude of optimism, happiness with small successes, and an emphasis on the future.
- Healing – This process is a person learning to identify himself as separate from the illness. Progress is made in overcoming or coping with the impact and daily effects of the disease. A person must regain a sense of control over his own life and repair self-esteem and confidence in his abilities.
- Empowerment – A person must feel in control of his life and the decisions that affect it. This stage is about taking back that control. Independence, self-determination, and strength are important.
- Connection – This is the process of fully reentering society and the larger community. It involves productivity, meaningful employment or occupation, social relationships, and independent living.

Stress

When reducing stress, one of the biggest environmental factors is uncertainty. Reducing or eliminating uncertainty can give stress relief. This might include obtaining clarification for vague instructions or guidelines, seeking specific information well in advance of an event such as location, dress code, arrival time, or determining a specific set of skills you will need. Another environmental factor that can reduce stress is mentally reducing the importance of an event. This can be accomplished by comparing it to other events you have already experienced or accomplished that are more important. Mental reminders that there will always be opportunities and mental exercise to focus on quality and completing an event rather than rewards or other people's reactions, can also help. Some individuals have found that listening to music or relaxation CD's prior to an event can be useful.

One physical technique for stress reduction is Progressive Muscular Relaxation (PMR). PMR teaches a person to contract a set of muscles as tightly as possible and hold it for several seconds. The person should let the muscles go back to inactive and then focus on relaxing the muscles as much as possible. This technique can be used with one muscle group or the entire body. Another physical technique is simple, controlled breathing in which the person focuses on taking a specific number of deep breaths and slow releases. Biofeedback is another technique helpful in reducing stress by promoting relaxation. Biofeedback uses electronic sensors to measure physical reactions such as skin temperature, heart rate, and muscle movement while individuals engage in specific activities including experimenting with stress reduction. This gives immediate insight into the effect of specific techniques and actions.

The body is designed to experience and deal with stress. However, if that stress is constant, with no break, physical health can be negatively affected. The body can begin to enter what is sometimes referred to as distress. This can produce negative physical symptoms such as headaches, stomach upset, difficulty sleeping, high blood pressure, unexplained rashes, and chest pain. Additionally, health conditions, disorders, or diseases can be aggravated by continuous stress. For example, diabetics might have greater difficulty regulating blood sugar, someone with chronic high blood pressure may no longer respond to previously effective treatments requiring medication changes or increases, and individuals with asthma may have increased attacks. Individuals experiencing continuous stress are also more likely to abuse substances in response, including alcohol, tobacco, and prescription drugs.

Focus of Self-Help Groups

Physical – this area focuses on getting all abused substances out of the body, coping with or overcoming the physical cravings for the substance, and getting physically healthy again

Psychological – this area focuses on no longer denying one's addiction, becoming emotionally stable, analyzing personal strengths and weaknesses, creating a desire to avoid addictive substances, forming a picture of one's identity separate from abuse, and forming a plan to stay free of substance abuse

Social – this area focuses on making up for past behavior that has harmed others, building new friendships and relationships that are supportive, identify life activities away from substance abuse, and correcting problems that were caused by the addiction

Spiritual – this area focuses on finding value and meaning in life, looking to a higher power for support, overcoming shame and guilt, and finding a way to assist others with problems

Important Terms

Extended Period of Eligibility (EPE): time after the trial work period in which an individual's right to continue to receive SSDI payments is determined by how much money is made on the job, presently this period is 36 consecutive months

Earned income exclusion: money that an individual makes that is not included in the Social Security Administration's determination of countable earned income

Trial work period: a period of nine months that do not have to be sequential during which an individual can get paid on the job and still receive SSDI payments in order to experiment with employment possibilities without risking government support

Substantial gainful activity (SGA): a specific amount of money made that the Social Security Administration considers evidence that an individual can support himself; presently this is $500 each month

1915(b) waiver: federal law that allows states to implement experimental programs that limit or eliminate individual freedom of choice in picking a health care provider, states can keep these programs in place for up to two years

1115 waiver: federal law that gives states great freedom in limiting individual choice in providers and health care services and even allows states to change Medicaid eligibility requirements, states must complete lengthy application process but can then keep state designed program in place for up to five years

Targeted case management: is a service that assists individual access to the services they need in a variety of areas including health care, vocational training, and social interaction; federal law allows Medicaid programs to provide this service to individuals with mental illness.

Mediation and Negotiation

Core Principles

- Always come prepared
- Keep it on a business level and do not let it become personal
- Keep emotions under control
- Confine all related conversation to private places and inform others on a need to know basis only
- Offers should include something for the other party because it cannot be unilateral
- Never reduce an offer before receiving a counteroffer from the other party
- Never make your final offer first without leaving room to maneuver
- Have other options so that you can walk away if necessary
- Sometimes it is necessary to take a chance
- Seek expert help when needed
- Do not overestimate the other party's resolve, resources, or commitment
- Use other language or labels to go after the same thing
- Do not rush negotiations or allow the other party to pressure with time
- The mediation atmosphere should be cooperative not confrontational
- Approach should be positive and focus on future improvement or success
- Outcomes should emphasize that there are no winners or losers
- The entire process should be voluntary in nature to foster acceptance for outcomes and any party can leave mediation at will
- All parties must have equal opportunities to be heard in a safe, respectful environment
- The process should emphasize complete honesty and openness from all parties
- Mediators should be completely impartial and remain neutral at all times
- Assurances of and adherence to confidentiality guarantees is vital
- Mediators should offer creative and original solutions

PAIMI Programs

PAIMI programs are free mental health advocacy programs available in all states. They provide services that protect the rights and safety of individuals with mental illness who are at risk for abuse or civil rights violations. PAIMI services can be obtained through individual request or complaints, initiated investigations, or second party requests. No matter how an individual is referred, PAIMI programs only represent the interests of the individual with mental illness. PAIMI representatives can seek solutions to problems on behalf of seriously ill individuals in hospitals or in-patient facilities by initiating hearings and if necessary, filing lawsuits. PAIMI often handle issues related to care given in private and public facilities as well as medication, treatments used such as seclusion and restraint, and consideration for individual choice and self-determination. This includes individual rights to privacy, choice in treatment options, least restrictive environment, and entitlement to certain benefits. Additional services include legal advice and assistance and referrals to other agencies. Individuals currently in hospitals, resident treatment facilities, and correctional institutions are given first priority. However, services have been expanded and are available to some individuals living in the community.

National Self-Help Groups

Dual Diagnosis Groups:

- Double Trouble in Recovery
- Dual Recoveries Anonymous
- Two Challenges and One Path Recovery Circle

12 Step Programs:

- We Can and Do Recover Circle
- Emotions Anonymous

Non 12 Step Programs:

- Depression and Bipolar Support Alliance
- Schizophrenics Anonymous
- Recovery, Inc.
- Wellness Recovery Circle

National Organizations that connect to local groups:

- National Mental Health Consumers' Self Help Clearinghouse
- National Empowerment Center
- Consumer Organization and Networking Technical Assistance Center
- American Self-Help Group Clearinghouse

Benefits of Self-Help Groups

- Access to a social network of individuals with common experiences to form new relationships and overcome stigma and isolation
- Assistance in moving from helplessness and dependence to self reliance and increased self-confidence
- Learning new coping strategies based on the failures and successes of others
- Escape from the constant structure and rigor of treatment in an environment of self-determination
- Improved interaction and productivity in society through increased confidence and effective coping skills
- The opportunity to function as a role-model for others by sharing experiences and wisdom
- Availability of a support network for times of crisis or relapse

Justice Department's Mediation Program

ADA (Americans with Disabilities Act) complaints are filed by individuals or groups who believe their rights under this law have been violated. Complainants can request mediation services to resolve the dispute. A mediator is provided by the Justice Department at no cost to either party. The goal of this program is to avoid the excessive costs associated with investigations and court proceedings. Mediation is non-binding until both parties sign an agreement and either party can abandon the mediation at any time prior to signing the agreement. If mediation does not work, a complainant can pursue other option including investigation and lawsuits. Although not guaranteed, the Justice Department tries to accommodate as many requests for mediation as possible. The request should be made when the formal complaint is filed.

Protection by ADA

The ADA prohibits discrimination by employers based on an individual's disability, including major mental illness. To qualify, the disability must be severe enough to interfere with a major life activity such as working, learning, and personal care. This law covers all aspects of the employment relationship including hiring, firing, promotion, benefits, salary, and recruitment. Employers are required to consider all qualified individuals equally, regardless of disability. If a disabled individual requires reasonable accommodations to be successful on the job, employers must provide them. Reasonable means that the cost is not excessive in comparison with the business production and they do not interfere with necessary business practices. Violations of individual rights under this law can be remedied by filing a complaint which initiates and investigation and legal action if needed.

Assessment, Planning, and Outcomes

Goals of Rehabilitation

The first goal of psychiatric rehabilitation, or PsyR, is helping those with major mental illnesses reach recovery. This requires the understanding that recovery is a unique experience for each person and the mental health professional is the guide on this path. PsyR professionals work with individuals to set and reach goals. The second major goal of PsyR is to help mentally ill individuals be as much a part of the mainstream community as possible. This includes some level of independent living as well as involvement and acceptance within the community. The third major goal of PsyR is helping individuals with mental illness experience life at the highest quality achievable. Issues related to this goal include basic aspects such as food, shelter, and clothing, but also apply to all the things that are important in life such as a job, relationships, sex, leisure activities, a support network, and a sense of community.

Assessment of Readiness

Readiness describes an individual's interest in and motivation to participate in psychiatric rehabilitation services. When conducting an assessment of readiness, a PsyR professional should consider the following factors:

- The interest level of the individual in pursuing change and/or the individual's level of unhappiness with his present situation
- The level of commitment the individual has to change, specifically the ideas that change has to happen and can happen, change can be positive, and support is available to assist this change
- The depth of understanding an individual has about the circumstances in which they which to be successful
- The understanding and knowledge that an individual has about himself, including strengths, values, beliefs, and personal preferences
- The level of trust that an individual has in the PsyR professional who will be providing services

Descriptors of Mental Illness

In an attempt to avoid labeling people with mental illness in a way that is derogatory, discriminatory, or demeaning, mental health professionals have devised alternate ways to describe the conditions or illnesses that the person is experiencing. The first descriptor is diagnosis. This involves giving a specific identity to the illness, such as schizophrenia or psychosis. The person would be described as having schizophrenia or psychosis, not as schizophrenic or psychotic. The second descriptor is the level of disability. This is usually in the form of commonly understood words such as mild, moderate, and severe. The third descriptor is duration. This indicates the length of time the person has suffered from the illness and/or the course it is taking. This might include wording such as ongoing, persistent, sporadic, prolonged, childhood, recent, etc.

SAMHSA's Description

- The individual has discussed, strategize about, or actually tried to commit suicide during the last year
- The individual has no meaningful or fruitful role within the community such as a job, volunteering, or attending school
- The individual has faced serious obstacles to his role within the community such as difficulty maintaining employment, obtaining housing, or accessing transportation
- The individual lacks any significant interaction or relationships with others or is isolated within the community

Beliefs About Recovery

- Recovery sometimes happens without any professional help because people are the most important ingredient in their own recovery
- A major factor in recovery is often the people an individual perceives as supporting and expressing confidence in them
- Recovery has nothing to do with a person's beliefs about the causes of psychiatric illnesses
- Recovery is not a cure and symptomatic episodes might happen, however recovery can happen without a cure
- Recovery alters the nature of symptomatic episodes in terms of length and reoccurrence
- Recovery is not a prescribed set of steps and does not follow a pattern
- Recovery from the effects of the disease such a loss of self-esteem and family estrangement, is sometimes the hardest part
- Recovery from psychiatric disorders should not be cause to negate the reality and seriousness of the illness

Diagnostic Stage

Readiness assessment – a tool to assist individuals in determining if they are ready to take part in rehabilitation

Readiness development – a variety of activities practitioners can provide individuals to increase readiness by expanding individual understanding about the rehabilitation process and demonstrating how rehabilitation can improve quality of life

Functional assessment – a tool that assists the PsyR practitioner and his client figure out what skills are needed to achieve the client's goals and which of these needed skills the client possesses

Resource assessment – a tool used in psychiatric rehabilitation to determine what support systems and other resources the client needs to achieve his goals and which of these are currently available

Intervention Stage

Direct skills teaching – an intervention utilized to develop lacking situational skills through activity-based instruction learning the skills in the target environment

Skills programming – an intervention utilized to help individuals take advantage of a skill they already possess by getting around obstacles to application in the target environment

Resource coordination – an intervention intended to support individuals by helping them identify and access resources and support systems that are available such as government programs, transportation systems, self-help programs, personal assistants, etc.

Resource modification – an intervention intended to support individuals by altering an available resource to better meet an individual's needs

Diagnosing and Planning

Diagnosing

- Determining if a client is prepared to participate in rehabilitation
- If unprepared for rehabilitation, assist client in reaching that point
- Establishing goals for rehabilitation by building a relationship with the client, helping the client determine interests and needs, assist client in considering environments in which he wishes to function
- Analyzing client's level of functioning by identifying needed skills and their various applications and determining the client's current skills and proficiency level
- Identify resources needed for client to reach goals and determine what resources are available, how they can help, and what is needed for the client to access those resources

Planning

- Establish a plan to build needed skills as well as to locate and access needed resources through determining most important needs, clarifying goals, and picking appropriate interventions with the client's help

Readiness Assessment Outcomes

The assessment might indicate that the client is prepared to start rehabilitation in which case they work together on the next step of establishing goals. The assessment might indicate that the client is not really prepared to begin rehabilitation, but he can still decide to proceed with starting the progress. In this case, the practitioner should help the client understand the rehabilitation may take more time to complete. If the assessment shows a lack of readiness, the client has many options to choose from including working with the practitioner on improving preparedness before entering rehabilitation to increase chances of success, delaying rehabilitation while focusing on treatment to manage symptoms, avoid rehabilitation services choosing other options such as self-help groups instead, or avoid all services completely.

Diagnostic Interview

Once the interview has been completed, the practitioner must organize the data gathered in a way that is productive to the overall goal. Guidelines for this will be different for each agency. In most situations, several important records will be created from the data including a readiness assessment, finalized goals for PsyR, and functional and resource assessments. Records should be clear with necessary detail, but also kept simple and relevant to the targeted environments. Readiness assessments must be designed using simple instruments such as 5-point scales or pre-formatted observations. The rehabilitation goals are often noted in a short, to-the-point statement at the beginning of the functional assessment. The functional assessment would identify the skills that are needed and specific situations that will require the skills and current level of skill mastery. This is often recorded as strengths and deficits. The resource assessment will list available resources and when access is needed.

Values Assessment

Values assessment is the process in which a practitioner gets a client to identify the things that he values in daily life. The practitioner works to make connections between client statements about values and objective daily goals. One technique that might be used with a client who is experiencing difficulty with this is a card sort. The practitioner makes a large number of cards labeled with many possible values such as "communicating positively with my family", "getting to work on time each day", or "finding someone in a romantic relationship". The practitioner provides the cards to the client with instructions to select those that fit his goals and sort them in order of importance. This activity can stimulate the client's own thoughts help him recognize additional goals not on the cards. Practitioners can also conduct values assessment in group therapy settings through discussion-based activities. The presentation of fictional or real dilemmas for consideration in individual or group settings can also be a technique to facilitate values assessment.

Advance Directives

An advance directive is written instructions on your preferences for treatment and care under certain medical circumstances. The area of advance directives for psychiatric care is very new and evolving. Personal preferences and wishes that might be addressed in an advance psychiatric directive include a legal and medical guardian in the case of incapacitation or declaration of incompetence, instructions about treatment including medications and use of options like restraint and electroconvulsive therapy, family notification instructions, prohibited and acceptable visitors, arrangements for care of minor children, and participation in experimental studies. Clients should always be advised to consult with a legal expert in the preparation of advance directives. Due to the emerging nature of this field, it is unclear how courts will respond to these directives. However, it does improve the chances that the legal system and medical professionals will respect individual wishes.

IAPSRS Outcomes Toolkit

The IAPSRS toolkit is an assessment tool designed to bring consistency and simplicity to the evaluation of programs serving individuals with mental illness. It is intended to measure the outcome of client goals and the effectiveness of interventions or programs. It does this by creating a database based on specified client outcomes. Outcomes are divided into seven domains or areas that coincide with the goals of psychiatric rehabilitation. These areas include employment, education or pursuit of education, housing situation, hospitalization, financial situation including income and receipt of entitlements, and legal matters. The toolkit also gathers demographic data and measures client perception in the areas of quality of life, personal empowerment, accomplishment of goals, and overall satisfaction with the program.

Outcome Measurement Tools

- Basic demographic information
- DSM-IV-TR diagnosis(s)
- Housing situation past, present, and targeted including support services utilized
- Hospitalization history including facility type and duration of stay
- Employment history including wages, hours, and support services utilized

- Education history including vocational training
- Government benefits and entitlements received
- Legal issues including arrests and imprisonment
- Overall member satisfaction with program with detailed surveys

EMPOWERMENT

Empowerment refers to the active and meaningful participation of individuals with mental illness in decisions affecting their lives. Empowerment gives a sense of control and power over one's life that is often missing for people suffering from mental illness. The principle of empowerment is recognized to be situational. Individuals might have greater power in some areas than others. Control can be exercise with the authority to make final decisions or might be shared with others. Empowerment can be seen in measurable, objective outcomes or in more subjective personal attitudes and perceptions. Empowerment cannot exist if it is given. People can support individuals seeking empowerment, but ultimately it must be taken for oneself. Support can be provided by ensuring individuals receive appropriate treatment to achieve a mental state that enables empowerment, making skills training available to facilitate personal choices and decisions, and guidance in accessing employment, housing, and other resources.

Assessment Tools

Diagnosis Confirmation

Structured Clinical Interview for DSM-IV-TR (SCID) – uses specific interview techniques to make psychiatric diagnoses from the DSM-IV-TR more dependable

Brief Psychiatric Rating Scale (BPRS) – is a rating scale that evaluates 18 items related to symptom severity used by a practitioner after interviewing a client

Symptom Checklist-90-R – is a 90-item assessment tool completed by the client to determine the severity and impact of psychiatric symptoms

Positive and Negative Syndrome Scale (PANSS), Scale for the Assessment of Positive Symptoms (SAPS), and Scale for the Assessment of Negative Symptoms (SANS) – helps identify certain sets or patterns of symptoms that correlate with specific disorders

Health Status

MOS 36 Item Short-Form Survey (SF 36) – evaluates social, behavioral, physical, and emotional aspects of health in people with chronic conditions or illnesses through an interview format or client self report

Sickness Impact Profile (SIP) – assesses illness related dysfunction in behavior terms by considering psychosocial and physical categories as well as measures of independent living

Quality of Well Being (QWB) – is a broad tool that can evaluate the effect of a specific system or program on the overall health situation of an individual or group

International Classification of Functioning and Disability – created by the WHO to consider disability of an individual by evaluating in the categories of functioning, behavior, and involvement in society

Global Functioning

Behavior and Symptom Identification Scale (BASIS-32) – is a 32-item tool completed by the client who asks for a rating of difficulty in a number of areas including relationships, daily living, functioning in desired roles, specific behaviors, level of depression or anxiety, and episodes of psychosis

Global Assessment of Functioning Scale (GAF) – is a single item rating on a scale of 0 to 100 based on a practitioners behavioral observations of client functioning in the areas of work, social interaction or involvement, and mental state

Disability Rating Form – measures level of disability on a five-point scale that correlates with the Social Security Administration's definition

Role Functioning Scale (RFS) – is a short tool that focuses on single measures for the four areas of independent living, occupational productivity, close social relationships, and expanded social interaction by measuring on a seven-point scale based on behavioral observations

Life Skills Profile (LSP) – schizophrenia-specific, 39 item tool that is completed by someone very familiar with the client to assess level of disability or functioning in the areas of caring for oneself, maintaining calm, social interaction, communication skills, and personal responsibility

Skills Measurement

Katz Adjustment Scale – this tool measures psychiatric symptoms, specific behaviors, and social adjustment skills such as managing money, completing chores, and getting along with others on a frequency scale that emphasizes client strength

Independent Living Skills Survey (ILSS) – this assessment measures daily living skills based on how often target behaviors occur according to the criteria of sometimes, often, never, usually, and always, as well as how often certain problems arise, and can be completed by a practitioner or a client

Community Competence Scale – this tool is administered in a semi-formal interview setting and covers topics in eighteen areas including managing money, nutrition, attention to general health, ability to make sound judgments, and social interaction

St. Louis Inventory of Community Living Skills – this tool evaluates very specific skills to determine how well a program is working, find appropriate placement, and measure skills acquisition based on documented behaviors, not predicted ability; measures areas such as cooking, cleaning, shopping, financial management, grooming, social relationships including sexuality, and problem solving

Social Environment

Social Performance Survey Schedule (SPSS) – this tool measures social skills and interaction based on how often identified behaviors occur and can be completed by the client or a close family member

Interpersonal Situation Inventory – measures client comfort level, on a five-point scale, in response to a variety of hypothetical social situations

Interpersonal Role-Playing Test (IRPT) – this tool uses situations from the Interpersonal Situation Inventory and requests client role playing in response, measuring the role playing on a scale of 0 to 2, with 2 demonstrating the minimum level of acceptable functioning in that scenario

Assessment of Interpersonal Problem Solving Skills (AIPSS) – this tool assesses social skills by showing a client video of dramatized problem situations and then asking the client to describe the problem, propose a solution, and act out the solution

Simulated Social Interaction Test (SSIT) – this assessment presents the client with eight hypothetical situations designed to produce anxiety and measures the client's responses and reactions while role playing in the situation

Important Terms

Goal: is a broad statement of a desired state one hopes to achieve, this should be the foundation of any psychiatric rehabilitation plan

Objective: is often considered a subordinate part of a broader goal, is usually more specific in nature with outcomes that can be measured, and may be more short term; a goal might be divided into a number of more specific objectives

Interventions: are actions, services, strategies, or products designed to help individuals overcome the effects of mental disability

Strength: is an identified ability, skill, or personal characteristic that an individual possesses, which can be used advantageously in recovery from psychiatric rehabilitation

Deficit: is an identified personal characteristic, lacking skill, or inability that inhibits recovery from psychiatric rehabilitation

Etiology: is the cause of an illness or disease

Prognosis: is the most likely path the disease or illness will follow and/or the end effect or result

Treatment - is anything done in an attempt to cure an illness or disease or to improve the negative symptoms

Rehabilitation: is anything done in an attempt to lessen the negative impact of an illness or disease on someone's daily life and activities

Chronic mental illness: is an ongoing or persistent disorder involving emotional, behavioral, and/or cognitive functions that is caused by genetic, environmental, or chemical factors or by injury

Positive symptoms: are things which start because of a disease or illness such as hearing voices

Negative symptoms: are things which stop because of a disease or illness such as the inability to enjoy the company of others

Psychosis: is a false sense of reality caused by inaccurate perceptions by the sensory system

Disability: is a mental or physical problem that interferes with a person's normal life activities or functions

Stage of recovery: describes how well a person is dealing with his illness, disease, or disability, his level of functioning, and his perception of himself

Functional assessment: determining what strengths and weaknesses an individual has in each circumstance in which they choose to participate and interact

Resource assessment: determining what resources are available to help and individual reach his goals including education or training, community programs, help with housing and transportation, and support systems

Rehabilitation plan: identifies what circumstances the individual will be pursing and what skills and resources are needed in those situations based on the choices of the individual and the functional assessment performed by the PsyR professional

Rehabilitation interventions: particular actions that will be taken to help the individual get the skills needed and access resources that are part of the rehabilitation plan

Interventions

Actions

- Offering direct skills teaching by detailing what skills will be taught, creating an instructional plan to engage the client in activities to learn the skill, and providing modeling and support during the entire process
- Offering skills use programming that assists the client in determining what obstacles are keeping him from successfully using skills, designing a plan to guide the client in using skills as desired in specific situations, and providing support during the entire process
- Coordinating resources for the client by providing education about all options, services, programs, and systems that are available, working with the client to resolve any issues related to accessing resources, and assist the client in choosing and maintaining specific resources that are most appropriate
- Modify resources to best meet the needs of the client by evaluating needed changes, suggesting modifications for the client's consideration, working as a liaison to resources and facilitate the change offering training if needed

Psychotropic Drugs Side Effects

- Irregularities with hormones
- Appetite changes
- Weight gain
- Muscular stiffness
- Poor motor coordination, especially noticeable when walking
- Dry mouth
- Vision problems such as blurring
- Altered blood pressure – usually low
- Seizures
- Symptoms similar to Parkinson's disease (usually reversible with discontinuation) such as tremors, difficulty controlling movement, shuffling walk
- Tardive dyskinesia (often irreversible even with discontinuation) – involuntary movements of the mouth, arms, or legs that has a strange appearance

Mikal Cohen's Principles

- Choose behavior reinforcement that will apply in a person's real life environment and use it during skills training
- Make sure that support is available to a person in his real life environment
- Anyone providing support should know how use rewards in a person's real life environment
- Move away from extrinsic rewards by helping the individual determine what motivates him
- Decrease dependence on reward for behavior by gradually lengthening time
- Give skills instruction in many different situations
- Expand skills by giving instructions in variations of the same skill
- Instruct individuals how to monitor their own progress and reward themselves
- Create true understand and deep learning by teaching clients the ideas or rules behind a skill

- Give outside assignments of increasing difficulty
- Emphasize self-determination by including the individual

The Clubhouse Movement

The clubhouse movement started in the 1940's as individuals with mental illness left hospitals and sought out the support and companionship of others with mental illness. This natural gravitating to one another was the result of societal stigma associated with their diseases. The first programs of this type were primarily social groups. However, these programs eventually evolved into a key factor in psychiatric rehabilitation. Members of these programs receive support and assistance from each other and mental health professionals in all areas of life including housing, employment, social and leisure activities, and access to available agencies and services. A primary focus of these programs is the value of work and how work leads to self confidence and independence. One of the first clubhouse programs was Fountain House in New York. Today, these programs exist in most major cities and some smaller communities.

Milieu Therapy

Milieu is a French word that means environment. The milieu therapy approach focuses on environment as the most important factor in treatment. All aspects of environment including cultural, social, and physical are considered in designing treatment. In these programs, all aspects of the day are designed to mimic real world situations. Special attention is given to creating an environment that while offering a real life feel, is also comfortable and inviting. Five specific characteristics are considered important in milieu therapy. First, clients should feel contained or managed by their environment. Next, the environment should feel supportive and uplifting. Structure is also important in providing a sense of order without unexpected events and surprises. Next, clients should experience a sense of acceptance and comfort in participating. Finally, the client should feel the environment personally confirms their value. Many PsyR professionals approve of this therapy as valuable for decreasing anxiety, making clients more cognizant of their own self, and facilitating positive behavior changes.

Day Program Characteristics

Clients must first be diagnosed with a major mental illness in order to participate in a PsyR day program. It should be considered if the program is the least restrictive environment that will serve the individual's needs. This usually indicates a past history of hospitalization as well as unsuccessful community integration without substantial support. If an individual currently has a high level of function in the community, a day program is not the least restrictive environment. Day programs are not appropriate for clients who could be dangerous to others or themselves. These individuals need a more restrictive environment such as a hospital. The environment of the day program should be considered as well as the tolerances of the client. The program will only be appropriate for clients for whom it is not unduly stressful.

Staff in a PsyR day program will include those who oversee and operate vocational programs, recreational activities, provide clinical supervision, and often medical staff. Support staff aide professionals in numerous capacities. These individuals will have training and/or education in the PsyR field. The level of education for support staff can start at high school extending to advanced academic degrees among supervisors, case managers, and other higher level staff. Education is usually in the areas of social work, psychology, and PsyR. The physical space of the program should be extensive enough to accommodate numerous separate activities and ideally have a large single space to hold all members of the program. The environment should be normal and the location safe and easy to get to using public transportation. Program activities can include job coaching, vocational training, social skills, medication management, recreational activities, remedial education such as GRE programs, education regarding client illnesses.

Based on professional observations and clinical research, it is clear that day programs are preferable to hospitalization for decreasing stigma and difficult transitions back into the community. These programs also allow individuals to maintain daily contact with family and other support people in their normal lives while at the same time, decreasing the burden illness places on the family. Research has shown that PsyR day programs combined with appropriate medications can significantly reduce the overall cost of treatment for mental illness by reducing the need for inpatient hospitalization. Day programs promote community integration and functioning through therapy, skills training, social skills, and positive support. Research has indicated that all programs are not effective and one important factor is tailoring the program to fit individual needs.

Case Management

Case management developed as a strategy to meet the needs of individuals with mental illness, living in the community, following the advance of deinstitutionalization. Although its meaning can vary widely, a generally accepted definition is any program or strategy that makes sure an individual gets all needed services in a timely and coordinated manner. Case managers focus on ensuring continuity of care, ease of access to services and programs, appropriate care from service agencies, and finding the services that are most appropriate to the client's needs, including financial needs. Meeting these needs means that a case worker has to develop a complete plan that involves determining individual needs and services available to meet those needs, setting goals, covering logistics for accessing the services, making sure the individual receives services with continual monitoring, and analyzing if services are appropriate on a continuous basis by monitoring progress toward goals.

- Offering direct skills teaching by detailing what skills will be taught, creating an instructional plan to engage the client in activities to learn the skill, and providing modeling and support during the entire process
- Offering skills use programming that assists the client in determining what obstacles are keeping him from successfully using skills, designing a plan to guide the client in using skills as desired in specific situations, and providing support during the entire process
- Coordinating resources for the client by providing education about all options, services, programs, and systems that are available, working with the client to resolve any issues related to accessing resources, and assist the client in choosing and maintaining specific resources that are most appropriate
- Modify resources to best meet the needs of the client by evaluating needed changes, suggesting modifications for the client's consideration, working as a liaison to resources and facilitate the change offering training if needed

MODELS

Rehabilitation Model – In this approach, case manager's focus on helping individuals with psychiatric disabilities set and reach goals in specific settings of their choice instead of created an all-encompassing plan. This process begins with the administration of function assessments in order to create a rehabilitation plan. The case manager supervises the client, supporting skills training, and helping the client build a support system in his chosen environment.

Personal Strengths Model – In this approach, also called the development-acquisition model, case managers work from two basic ideas: success requires a person to utilize their own potential and access needed resources and how a person behaves is determined by the resources they have. From this perspective, case managers emphasize an individual's strengths rather than their overall makeup and guide them to develop their own problem solving skills and locate needed resources. This model is most consistent with PsyR philosophy.

Full support case management, also referred to as ACT or TCL, is an approach that seeks to supply all the support and services that an individual with psychiatric disability needs. This approach was created as an approach to psychiatric rehabilitation that emphasized the importance of keeping clients from being hospitalized or re-hospitalized. This approach designs an all-encompassing system of support that is available to clients at any time and any place. TCL starts with an individual plan for each client. Services are provided by a team of experts in every area from medical care and counseling to vocational training and are offered to the client at home, work, school, or leisure. Paying close attention to an individual's plan, staff members focus on providing support in any area that is likely to precipitate a setback requiring hospitalization. 24-hour crisis intervention is available as a short in-patient stays if needed. Support extends from ensuring basic services are available such as housing and food to job training and placement, on the job support, medication monitoring and counseling.

Promoting Self-Help Initiatives

The first step is staff encouragement of social interaction between individuals in a psychiatric rehabilitation program with the goal of increasing individual concern for the fellow members. The next step is increasing client involvement in their own treatment including planning activities and choosing from several options. During this step, some clients will show leadership qualities, which should be encouraged through greater responsibility, supervision opportunities, and teaching roles. The third step involves openness and even rebellion among clients about their situation. Concerns will be expressed about elements of the program, certain staff members, level of personal control, and choices available to clients. Staff members should encourage conversation and provide clients with available information about self-help groups. During the next step, roles begin to change as clients assume greater responsibility for their lives. Meetings might be held away from the program and clients might assign themselves new labels. In the last step, clients take the step of formally created a self-help group. Staff members should continue to offer support on an as-needed basis.

Self-Help Groups and MICA

MICA stands for Mentally Ill Substance Abuser. This dual diagnosis presents an especially difficult challenge for treatment options. Mental health professionals often suggest that clients receiving services also access community self help groups. Two commonly suggested organizations are Alcoholics Anonymous (AA) and Narcotics Anonymous (NA). Individuals with mental illness are sometimes stigmatized even within these groups where people fear or misunderstand their condition. These two groups also discourage the use of psychiatric medications as addictive, interfering with treatment plans. In response, recent years have seen the creation of new groups, known as double trouble groups, which are designed to help people diagnosed as MICA. These programs often follow protocol similar to AA and NA with the exception of promoting adherence to medication plans and greater acceptance of individuals experiencing a variety of psychiatric symptoms.

Factors Influencing Health

At a basic level, every person is by several factors beyond our control: age, gender, ethnicity, and heredity. Every person is also influenced by lifestyle choices that are usually within our control. This can include habits such as smoking or drinking, exercise level, sexual practices, sleeping, and risk-seeking or avoidance. Research also suggests that relationships, social interactions, and community play some role in overall health. On a broader level are socio-economic, environmental, and cultural factors that may or may not be controllable, also influence health. This includes housing, living conditions, availability and choice in food and nutrition, employment or lack of employment, education, water sources, sanitation, and access to healthcare. While individuals cannot control certain factors, each person must be aware of those elements that are controllable and impact overall health.

Health Belief Model

This model for health promotion is based on the behavioral concept that a person will only change if there is an incentive to change. This could be a threat of danger or loss or it could be the perception that change will benefit the person in some way and is affordable. For any change to take place the person must also feel he can facilitate the change or access the resources to change. From a health perspective, an individual must be enlightened regarding the specific risks of illnesses, diseases, and related factors. He must also be educated on the benefits of pursuing specific treatments or engaging in certain behaviors. This education must be combined with reassurances of individual competence to perform behaviors and guidance in accessing needed resources such as medical care, medications, nutrition training, and improved living conditions.

Bruce Tuckerman's stages

Tuckerman proposed that the optimal group formation happens in four distinct stages. *The first stage is called forming*. During forming, group members maintain surface politeness and pretend to get along and agree. *The next stage is called storming*. During storming, group members try to approach issues more realistically and begin sharing more honestly, even if it means conflict within the group. *The next stage is norming*, during which members are increasingly comfortable with one another. Trust begins to grow between group members and more is accomplished. *The fourth stage is known as conforming or performing*, when group dynamics are productive. Group activities emphasize cooperation and can focus on a common goal. Tuckerman later added a *fifth stage to his theory of group dynamics called adjourning*, to describe when a group breaks apart.

Kurt Lewin's Theories

Lewin conducted extensive field research in group dynamics and generated several key observations. The first is the impact of democratic leadership. He discovered that groups with democratic leadership exhibited more cooperation, group unity, friendly attitudes, and creativity when compared to groups with autocratic or hands-off leadership. Another key observation was what Lewin described as the phenomenon of interdependence of fate. When group members recognized their common goal, or that each member's success depended on the others, groups were more productive. A third observation is the impact of what Lewin calls task interdependence. If one member cannot successful complete a task without the help of another, productivity and likelihood of success are increased.

Group Cohesion Factors

Typically, the smaller a group's size, the more quickly cohesion develops. In very large groups, cohesion may never fully emerge.

Commonality – Cohesion develops more quickly if group members have characteristics in common. This could include age, gender, occupation, or medical condition. These factors can contribute to a sense of common purpose.

Stability – Cohesion increases over time when a group maintains the same members. Introduction of new members or departure of original members can impact cohesion.

Happiness – The level of happiness that group members experience with each other, group goals and accomplishments, and adherence of all members to group norms, impacts overall cohesion.

Support/Leadership – Groups with external support and/or good leadership have greater cohesion.

Interventions

General Guidelines

Involuntary interventions are those which are implemented without client approval and consent and even, in some cases, against the individual's wishes. These actions are legal permissible under certain conditions. Laws vary from state to state on the use of involuntary interventions, but some general guidelines usually apply. If an individual is in danger of being significantly harmed, an involuntary intervention is appropriate if a reasonable person could not prefer the harm to the intervention. Additionally, consideration should be given to any potential reason the individual might have for wanting to suffer the harm. Unless adequate reason can be found, involuntary intervention can be justified. The third guideline to consider is the likelihood that the involuntary intervention will prevent the imminent harm.

Warning Signs for Relapse

- Discontinuing psychiatric medications without advice of a doctor
- Isolating oneself and avoiding appointments and rehabilitation related meetings
- Overconfidence in one's ability to function without support
- Significant relationship problems
- Hanging out with friends who still drink or abuse drugs
- Experiencing major life changes such as death, loss of a job, or inheriting a large amount of money
- Abandoning rehabilitation treatment plan
- Sudden onset of psychiatric symptoms after a period of recovery
- Changes in appearance, personal grooming, or eating habits
- Inability to move forward and focus on past events
- Refusal to deal with ordinary, daily problems
- Establishing unrealistic goals and placing excessive pressure on oneself

Involuntary Interventions

Protection of people and property – This category covers actions and programs designed to protect the welfare of an individual and care for his property and possessions. This can include government entitlement programs to provide basic necessities such as Supplemental Security Income and Social Security Disability. It can also involve the establishment of legal trusts or the assignment of legal guardianships to care for the well being of impaired individuals.

Mandates on treatment – Under certain conditions which vary from state to state, individuals might be forced to receive certain treatments such as involuntary commitment, hospitalization, medications, or participation in therapy when released from residential treatment.

Orders stemming from illegal actions – Individuals with mental illness might have treatment or rehabilitation mandated as part of legal actions resulting from criminal charges, criminal convictions, parole, or probation orders. This could include housing and employment specifications, mandatory vocational training, medication compliance, therapy, and in or out patient services.

Mental Health Courts

Mental health courts, sometimes referred to as problem solving courts, have been created to address the unique needs of individuals with mental illness who have become defendants within the justice system. These courts recognize the role mental illness plays in criminal activity and seek to reduce repeat offenses as well as obtain needed services for those with mental illness. Participation in these courts is voluntary and conducted with full disclosure and information for the individual. The courts seek to coordinate between law enforcement, judicial agencies, mental health and advocacy groups, and the individual and his family. The courts develop an individual plan for each defendant that balances the person's needs with concerns for public safety. In addition to satisfying society's demands for justice when laws have been broken, the courts facilitate access to support services in mental health treatment, vocational programs, housing, and other supports. Defendants might receive less stringent punishments and appropriate care is emphasized. Individuals are held accountable through judicial monitoring and conditions can change as warranted.

Problem Solving Process

The first step is problem orientation. This involves accepting the reality of an existing problem and determining that it is worth the time to solve it. At this stage it is important to get in the right frame of mind, finding confidence and will power to overcome the problem. The next step is defining the problem. The problem may be more complex or slightly different that is first perceived. This means gathering information and considering it carefully to be sure the real problem has been identified. If multiple problems are present, prioritize and start with the first one. The third step is to generate multiple solutions to the problem. This involves brainstorming about possible options and considering what past actions might be applicable with this problem. All solutions should be considered, no matter how extreme or unlikely to succeed. The next step is to narrow down the options that were generated and choose one solution. This involves considering pros and cons as well as the likelihood of success for each option. Issues that might be considered are realism, cost, involvement of others, limits on resources or skills, time needed, and difficulty. The final step is to move forward with the choice and monitor its success, back stepping to consider other options if needed.

Anthony and Liberman's Model

This model offers a theory about the cause of major mental illness and how it can be impacted by support systems, rehabilitation, and treatment. According to this model, individuals can be predisposed to mental illness through heredity or other area of susceptibility. The illness can be brought on by external factors such as death of a loved one or major transitions like moving or marriage. Physical factors such as disease, traumatic injury, or severe illness can also trigger the mental illness. This model suggests that an individual's reaction and response to these triggers is highly influenced by support systems and personal coping skills that are in place at that time. Strong personal coping skills and access to strong natural, community, and professional support reduce the impact of the illness which can be seen in milder symptoms, shorter duration of relapse, fewer incidents of relapse, and greater ability to continue functioning in a normalized environment.

Important Terms

Acute phase: The stage during which a disease is most noticeable and its symptoms are the most extreme.

Biological treatment: A medical approach to addressing the disease or minimizing symptoms that utilizes medications.

Decompensation: When an individual cannot sustain a balanced state generally avoiding symptoms.

Depressive episode: A period of time of at least 14 days during which an individual experiences feelings of overwhelming sadness or loss for most or all of each day.

Delusions: Inaccurate ideas that an individual refuses to give up even though there is no evidence to prove the ideas and possibly even evidence to contradict it.

Manic episode: A period that can last a week or longer in which the individual experiences a raised or high mood

Empowerment: Is a sense of control over one's life built on the elements of self-esteem, confidence in one's abilities, positive outlook, and an active role in the present and future.

Hallucinations: An individual senses the presence of sounds, objects, or situations that are not there.

Mixed episode: Includes both manic and depressive episodes that alternate

Residual phrase: The time after an acute phase of the disease when symptoms subside or lessen.

Prodromal phrase: The time prior to the disease becomes full blown when an individual starts to experience difficulty functioning and symptoms appear and/or increase.

Double trouble: Self help groups offering support and tiered programs to individuals with a dual diagnosis of mental illness and substance abuse.

Family foster care: A residential environment where one or more individuals with mental illness live with a family other than their own.

Individual written rehabilitation plan (IWRP): A formalized statement jointly developed between client and practitioner that identifies the employment goals and resources that will be utilized to reach it.

Psychoeducation: An intervention strategy in which the mental health practitioner partners with the client's family to build a rehabilitation partnership and increase support for the client, accomplished through communication, education, training, and resource identification.

Reasonable accommodations: Changes in a work environment that help a worker with a disability such as mental illness function effectively but do not place an excessive financial burden on the employer or negatively impact the business function and performance.

Diversity

Labels

Individuals who are institutionalized, or in a hospital, are usually referred to as patients. Those people who live in the community and receive mental health services from a community or private center are usually called clients. Some day programs like the Clubhouse philosophy might refer to their participants as members. Some individuals live in full time residential centers and receive mental health services. These people are commonly called residents. Some people with mental illness resent the labels that society has imposed and might develop their own labels, such as consumer, since they consume mental health services, or even prosumer to describe their cooperative relationship with mental health professionals. Some call themselves survivors to mark their co-existence with the disease.

Using Dignified Language

There are many labels commonly used to refer to individuals with mental illness. If labels are used, they should be those that are most acceptable to those with illness. Currently this includes referring to mentally ill as "people with psychiatric disabilities" or "persons with severe mental illness". A common mistake to be avoided is placing more emphasis on the disease or condition than on the person himself. This means that a person should be described as "someone with schizophrenia" rather than a "schizophrenic". Language should be used that does not place excessive emphasis on a person's disability or disease, but rather focuses on their humanity and importance as a person. Since patient refers to someone in a hospital, doctor's office, or medical setting, that word should be avoided when working with people receiving psychiatric rehabilitation.

Asian Background Considerations

Since the mental health system in the United States is a product of the influence of white, European ancestry, some Asians feel uncomfortable with the system's values and the majority of mental health professionals from this background. Asian culture has a tendency to exhibit great willpower and feel pressure to avoid upsetting or disrupting others. The culture places great emphasis on social harmony. Problems are sometimes viewed differently with much weight given to the need for balance such as the ying/yang or hot/cold beliefs. Asian culture also avoids focusing or dwelling unnecessarily on issues related to death, illness, or anything troubling. Avoiding these topics is valued over recognition, discussion, and acceptance. There is greater stigma within Asian culture for mental illness than among other groups and this is connected the cultural emphasis on saving face. This can not only inhibit seeking professional help, but also turning to family members for support. This group has the lowest statistical level for seeking professional help for mental illness.

Somatization is the presentation of mental illness as physical symptoms. This is much more common is Asian cultures than is Western cultures, possibly due to the higher prevalence of stigma associated with mental illness as well as the Asian perspective on mind and body as one entity. Common physical symptoms reported include sensations of lumps or heaviness in the throat, shortness of breath, stomach upset or chronic indigestion, headaches, dizziness, fatigue, and generalized pain or weakness. Cognitive disruption such as difficulty concentrating and memory loss are often reported as well as sexual dysfunction, sleep disorders, and changes in eating habits. Medical tests must be used to rule out actual physical disorders and practitioners must question clients about use of herbs and non prescription treatments that are culturally prevalent.

African-American Considerations

Since the mental health system in the United States is a product of the influence of white, European ancestry, some African-Americans feel uncomfortable with the system's values and the majority of mental health professionals from this background. There is also a strong sense of distrust for these macro culture dominated systems and an enhanced perception of racism or racial slights. Some of this is only perceived, but practitioner bias does exist and inhibit treatment. African-Americans might first turn to community churches and family members for help when facing mental illness. This group has a strong reliance on extended family support systems. This can be valuable, but only when combined with professional services which many do not seek. Statistics seem to indicate a higher incidence of mental illness proportionately among African-Americans, connected to lower socioeconomic status. Economic status can also impede lower income African-Americans from accessing available services. There is a tendency, especially among the uninsured, to use emergency room services rather than more specialized treatment options. This is often inadequate for diagnosing or treating mental illness.

Statistics indicate that African Americans are more likely to experience major depression and suffer from phobias than Caucasians. Onset of physical illness as a result of mental illness is also more common in African Americans than in whites. Research supports metabolic differences between whites and African Americans in processing medications, with African Americans metabolizing some medications much slower. This can have a significant impact on therapeutic effects and side effects, yet differentiation in dosing is often overlooked. This also increases the chance that individuals will choose to discontinue medications. Statistics indicate African Americans are disproportionately present in situations that have been linked to higher rates of mental illness. This includes homelessness, foster care, and correctional facilities. Some research points to inequalities in mental health treatment for African Americans. Studies have shown lower rates of accurate diagnoses with presenting with similar symptoms as compared to whites and lower prescriptions rates for newer, more effective SSRI medications.

Hispanic Considerations

Since the mental health system in the United States is a product of the influence of white, European ancestry, some Hispanics feel uncomfortable with the system's values and the majority of mental health professionals from this background. The Hispanic community places great value on family and church and often individuals will access these resources without seeking professional help for mental illness. The lower economic status of many individuals in this group often leaves them uninsured and seeking medical care from emergency rooms or free clinics where appropriated diagnosis and treatment for mental illness are unlikely. This is especially true of recent immigrants. Language barriers can often prevent Hispanics from seeking treatment or receiving appropriate treatment and there is strong community stigma attached to mental illness.

Hispanic somatic syndromes and complaints brought on by mental illnesses that are common to Hispanic cultures:

- Attack of nerves – Characterized by panic attacks accompanied by violent behavior, uncontrollable shouting, fainting, and pseudo-seizures.
- Milder nervous state – Characterized by mood variations, emotional distress, nervousness or restlessness, stomach discomfort, and often aggravated by environmental factors.
- State of fright or susto – Described by individuals as the soul leaving the body due to fear or trauma and characterized by anxiety, profuse sweating, eating disorders, irregular heartbeat, and stomach disorders; cultural tendency to rely on spiritualists.
- Occasional isolated psychotic symptoms with no other presenting symptoms of mental illness – Unusual auditory or visual hallucination such as a doorbell ringing, a child's voice calling, or seeing shadows where others do not.

Western Viewpoints on Confidentiality

In western medicine and therapy, client or consumer confidentiality is considered one of the highest priorities. Involving family members in a client's treatment or client's rehabilitation would be conditional on the individual's express written approval. Indicative of our individualistic society, in many situations, practitioners will not even initiate this involvement of others in a client's treatment or services. In other cultures, confidentiality is seen to include the immediate family members. Within our own culture confidentiality can limit the success of treatment and rehabilitation if family members providing care-giving services are not fully informed and involved in all processes. African-American, Hispanic, and Asian families are more likely than whites to keep individuals with mental illness at home rather than residential or community living centers.

Conflicting Norms

- In Latin American cultures it is typical for clients to present doctors or medical professionals with small gifts to show gratitude. This conflicts with most American ethics codes for medical practitioners which forbid the acceptance of any gifts or favors from clients. However, refusal of such gifts would be highly insulting to individuals from those cultures.
- In some Asian and Middle Eastern cultures, families will make financial arrangements to "purchase" a spouse for a mentally ill family member. While this seems very unusual and might be labeled unhealthy by many western medical professionals, it is often satisfactory to all parties involved in those cultures.
- Many cultures outside the mainstream have healing practices that conflict with western medicine or may be viewed with skepticism or contempt by western medical practitioners. Individuals from these cultures might seek dual treatment from within their own traditions while accessing western treatments. Examples of these healing systems include Brazilian umbanda, Haitian vodou, Native American medicine, Caribbean obeah, and Mexican curanderismo.

Cultural Elements of Assessment

- Initial and subsequent assessment must consider cultural factors that can impact treatment or rehabilitation success such as language preference, religious affiliation or beliefs, history of immigration or movement, social network and family supports, learning styles, extent of acculturation, education levels, ethnic identity, gender and sexual orientation, personal belief systems regarding mental illness, economic factors, and history of discrimination.
- Bilingual staff or outside interpreters with linguistic and cultural knowledge must be present for all assessments if needed.
- Assessment categories and items must be culturally valid and should be interpreted by professionals with cultural proficiency.
- Assessment must distinguish between indicators which are biological, pathological, or disease related, and those which are cultural such as eye contact avoidance, speech and cognitive patterns, and social relationships.

Researchers and practitioners have raised concerns about the validity of standardized assessments when used to evaluate certain minority cultures such as African Americans or those of Latino background. The main concern is the potential for cultural bias in the question structure, question type, and interpretation of results. One commonly used test in assessing psychiatric illness is the MMPI-2. It is favored by practitioners because of its high reliability in screening for misrepresentation of symptoms. Researchers have observed that African Americans often show more indications of exaggerations of symptoms than white clients. Closer examination suggests this could be tied to socioeconomic status. IQ tests are another area of concern with Latino and African American clients who score 10 more points lower than white clients on average. Researchers have suggested the influence of historical experience, cultural beliefs, and innate problem solving skills unique to cultural experience. Practitioners should use caution when interpreting results to avoid cultural miscues that interfere with accurate diagnoses.

Arthur Kleinman's Questions

The following questions, developed by Arthur Kleinman, assist practitioners in considering mental illness from a client's perspective. By better understanding the client's views about the illness, the practitioner can suggest treatment plans and interventions that are complimentary to the client's cultural and personal belief system.

- What do you call your problem?
- What do you think caused your problem?
- Why do you think it started when it did?
- What does it do to you?
- How severe is it?
- What do you fear most about it? The main problems it has caused you?
- What kind of treatment do you think you should receive?

Attitudes or Beliefs Prevalent in the African American Community, Which Can Impact Treatment for Mental Illness and Possible Practitioner Approaches Towards These Attitudes

Many African Americans receiving treatment for mental illness express concerns about prolonged use of medications and indicate fears of addiction. Practitioners can discuss the addictive properties of medications to be considered and offer alternative medications. If indicated, practitioners can also offer alternative treatment options such as psychotherapy. Emphasis on spirituality and religion within the African American community can delay treatment as individuals seek help from individuals and organizations within the church. By the time these individuals turn to medical professionals for help, difficulty in treatment might have increased significantly. Practitioners should assess the role of religion and church in clients' lives and encourage accessing that natural support system. Many African American individuals have expressed distrust of non-African American practitioners. This can limit opportunities for treatment, especially among low socioeconomic segments of the population served by free clinics or community services. Practitioners can educate themselves and staff members about cultural sensitivity in treating clients.

Assessment Validity for Minorities

Researchers and practitioners have raised concerns about the validity of standardized assessments when used to evaluate certain minority cultures such as African Americans or those of Latino background. The main concern is the potential for cultural bias in the question structure, question type, and interpretation of results. One commonly used test in assessing psychiatric illness is the MMPI-2. It is favored by practitioners because of its high reliability in screening for misrepresentation of symptoms. Researchers have observed that African Americans often show more indications of exaggerations of symptoms than white clients. Closer examination suggests this could be tied to socioeconomic status. IQ tests are another area of concern with Latino and African American clients who score 10 more points lower than white clients on average. Researchers have suggested the influence of historical experience, cultural beliefs, and innate problem solving skills unique to cultural experience. Practitioners should use caution when interpreting results to avoid cultural miscues that interfere with accurate diagnoses.

Important Terms

Alternative healer (folk healer): A person who is valued within a community or culture based on acquired knowledge and training in treating ailments through the use of non-medical techniques such as herbs, rituals, spirituality, and counseling.

Bicultural: The ability to comprehend and interact effectively in two or more unique cultures, but does not always demonstrate cultural competence.

Culturally appropriate: The ability of a person or group to address the health and behavior of specific cultural groups through ongoing improvement of services and programs that meet the cultural and linguistic needs of that group.

Cultural assessment: Part of the assessment process involving practitioners, clients, and client family and support systems in which cultural factors are considered for relevance to treatment.

Cultural compatibility: The availability of programs, services, and support personnel that bring in cultural components such as language, history, beliefs, values, and behavior patterns of individuals in the cultural group being served.

CPRP Practice Test

Want to take this practice test in an online interactive format?
Check out the online resources page, which includes interactive practice questions and much more: **mometrix.com/resources719/cprp**

1. Which of the following is NOT a quality that should be found in a psych rehab program?

a. Individualization
b. Disease-oriented care
c. Confidence in the clients to be successful in the program
d. Focus towards normalization of each client

2. What is the goal of a psych rehab center?

a. To manage the symptoms of the client's mental illness
b. To get the clients to comply and live within the rules of the rehab center
c. To get a job
d. To set and achieve reasonable goals for clients to work toward being productive members of society

3. One of the most common positive symptoms of schizophrenia is:

a. Delusions
b. Avolition
c. Anhedonia
d. Flat affect

4. The characteristic symptoms of schizophrenia are most notable and bothersome during which phase?

a. Prodromal
b. Primary
c. Acute
d. Tertiary

5. A client presenting with a dual diagnosis commonly has a mental illness and a:

a. Developmental disability
b. Seizure disorder
c. Second mental illness
d. Physical disability

6. Which of the following is an example of a subjective burden?

a. Inability of a family member to travel
b. Financial difficulties related to cost of care
c. Providing for an ill family member who is unable to work
d. Differing opinions on the type of care a family member needs

7. Family members who are less involved in the day-to-day care of the psychiatric client but who are more likely to be affected by a relapse are called:

a. First-tier family members
b. Second-tier family members
c. Third-tier family members
d. Fourth-tier family members

8. Who should be involved in the development of client treatment goals in a psychiatric rehab program?

a. The client and the psych rehab practitioner
b. The client, their family, and the psych rehab practitioner
c. The client's family and the psych rehab practitioner
d. Only the psych rehab practitioner

9. Family members often report feelings of sadness or grief during which phase of recovery?

a. First
b. Second
c. Third
d. Fourth

10. Which of the following is NOT an appropriate way for the family of a client to become educated about the client's condition?

a. Speaking with the client's roommate about how he or she is doing
b. Attending a survival skills workshop
c. Finding a support group especially for families of mentally ill clients
d. Consulting with the staff and the client's psych rehab counselor

11. Which of the following strategies would NOT follow the GRACE method?

a. Empathize with the individual to encourage trust and honesty
b. Be confident in the individual's ability to make the necessary changes
c. Push the client to move at an accelerated pace to encourage progress
d. Work with his/her resistance by allowing the individual to observe both the positive and negative points

12. Albert Bandura created which of the following?

a. The GRACE strategy for communication
b. Social Learning Theory
c. Communication Competence Theory
d. Interactional View Theory

13. Which of the following is true of biological treatment of mental illness?

a. The goal of using medication is to cure the disease
b. It should not be used during a crisis situation
c. It is more effective in managing negative symptoms
d. It is more effective in managing positive symptoms

14. Which of the following is NOT true of psychiatric recovery?

a. An important step is acceptance of the mental illness
b. The client understands that setbacks and relapses may occur
c. True recovery results in lifelong freedom from symptoms and a return to normal functioning
d. Each client has his or her own definition of and path to recovery

15. To help individuals maintain new skills, PsyR professionals should:

a. Provide frequent instruction about relevant skills
b. Give clients ample time to role-play new skills
c. Allow the client to practice their new skills in actual real-world situations
d. Trust that family members will also assist in helping the client practice new skills

16. What is required for Client-Centered Therapy to work?

a. A therapist with a strong and defined viewpoint
b. A relationship between client and therapist that is based on mutual respect and trust
c. A client whose condition is in remission
d. Clear positive and negative reinforcement

17. Which of the following is true of supported employment programs?

a. The program is covered by the Federal Rehabilitation Act
b. A group of 10 to 15 employees work in the group at a time
c. A job coach checks in with the group once a week
d. Each member of the group chooses the job that he or she likes to do within the company

18. Employer education involves:

a. Addressing employer needs and educating employers about the contributions that people with mental illness can make
b. Training employees about available support systems
c. Educating employers about risks involved in hiring people with mental illness
d. Training employees about how to work with people with mental illness

19. Which of the following is a disadvantage of living in a boarding home?

a. Expensive
b. Often leads to hospitalization
c. Too much privacy can lead to dangerous behaviors
d. Potential for abuse

20. A client who is at risk for medication noncompliance and who needs additional support with activities of daily living would be best suited to live in which living facility?

a. Boarding home
b. Fairweather lodges
c. Residential treatment center
d. At home with daily visits to a day program

21. The Fair Housing Act:

a. Prevents discrimination against people with disabilities, but there are no provisions for people with mental illness
b. Allows landlords to have different renting requirements for individuals with disabilities
c. Prohibits landlords from refusing to rent apartments to individuals with mental illness
d. Is enforced by the local housing agency

22. Under HIPAA, medical information CANNOT be shared with:

a. Family members, regardless of the client's request
b. The client's insurance company
c. Governing agencies when the information could protect public health
d. His or her employer

23. Which of the following federal programs covers hospitalization in a specialized psychiatric facility for 190 days in a lifetime?

a. Medicaid
b. Medicare Part A
c. Medicare Part B
d. Medicare Part C

24. Which of the following should NOT be a factor that indicates a client is ready to enter a psych rehab program?

a. The level of commitment that the client's family exhibits
b. The degree of trust that the client has towards the PsyR staff
c. The interest and level of commitment that the client has in making positive changes
d. Whether the client has insight into his situation and what is required of him

25. A functional assessment is a tool used by practitioners to:

a. Assess what skills the client would like to gain
b. Determine the skills that the client has and which ones she needs to work on
c. Identify the resources the client has available to him
d. Assess the job that the client would be most suited for

26. Which of these tools should only be used for assessing clients with schizophrenia?

a. Role Functioning Scale
b. Disability Rating Form
c. Life Skills Profile
d. Behavior and Symptom Identification Scale

27. The Simulated Social Interaction Test:

a. Uses 8 hypothetical situations that are stress-inducing and are used to test the client's response
b. Uses videos of problems that have been acted-out to have the client describe the problem and potential solutions
c. Utilizes a five-point scale to measure the client's degree of comfort with certain situations
d. Uses a two-point scale to judge a client's role-played response on appropriateness and acceptability of behavior

28. The etiology of a syndrome is:

a. The most likely outcome
b. Anything that is done to attempt to cure the syndrome
c. An action taken to lessen the effect of a disease on a client's activities of daily living
d. The cause of the disease

29. A client with schizophrenic presents to a psychiatric rehab program alone. Which assessment tool should be deferred until a family member or close friend can be present?

a. Simulated Social Interaction Test
b. Life Skills Profile
c. Community Competence Scale
d. Katz Adjustment Scale

30. When working with a client on advance directives, the client should always be advised that:

a. They should consult with an attorney or legal expert
b. Their wishes will likely not be upheld because their ability to give consent may be questionable
c. There is no protocol for advance directives for psychiatric care
d. The directives will only cover emergency medical care

31. After interviewing a client for his initial assessment and reviewing his chart (diagnosis included), you want to determine how severe his psychiatric symptoms are. Which checklist should you use?

a. Scale for the Assessment of Positive Symptoms
b. Scale for the Assessment of Negative Symptoms
c. Brief Psychiatric Rating Scale
d. Sickness Impact Profile

32. Which of the following is NOT an expected side effect of psychotropic drugs?

a. Changes in appetite
b. Weight gain
c. Rapid heart rate
d. Tardive dyskinesia

33. Milieu therapy focuses on:

a. The client
b. The environment
c. The therapist
d. The mental illness

34. Which model of case management would be most appropriate for a client who needs complete support because of frequent relapses and hospitalizations?

a. Training in community living (TCL)
b. Crisis management
c. Personal strengths
d. Rehabilitation

35. Double Trouble groups are most useful for clients with what condition(s)?

a. Narcotics and alcohol addiction
b. Two mental health illnesses
c. Mental illness within multiple family members
d. Both mental illness and drug/alcohol addiction

36. From the perspective of the Health Belief Model, clients will only make positive changes if:

a. They have a strong family system
b. Their health is in danger
c. They receive prompt medical and psychiatric attention
d. There is sufficient motivation to make the change

37. According to Bruce Tuckman's four stages of group development, storming occurs when:

a. Members of the group begin to approach issues more honestly, regardless of the potential for conflict
b. The group breaks up
c. The members of the group feel increasingly more comfortable with each other
d. A point is reached where they are able to work productively

38. Which of the following statements about mental health courts is INCORRECT?

a. They are used to manage the unique needs of people with mental illness
b. Participation can be mandated by the legal system
c. Less stringent punishments may apply
d. The courts can provide additional access to support services as part of their recommendation

39. The prodromal phase of mental illness occurs when:

a. When the disease is most noticeable and the symptoms most problematic
b. The time immediately after an acute crisis situation
c. When the client begins to have difficulty functioning right before the active phase of the disease
d. When the active phase of the syndrome is in remission.

40. The main difference between Social Security Disability Insurance (SSDI) and Supplemental Security Income (SSI) is that:

a. SSDI is not funded by taxpayer contributions
b. SSI requires that you have paid into the Social Security system to be eligible for benefits
c. SSDI benefits are paid out immediately upon becoming disabled
d. SSDI requires that you have paid into the Social Security system to be eligible to receive benefits

41. A 1915(b) waiver allows states to:

a. Limit client choice of health care providers and medical services
b. Change SSI eligibility requirements depending on availability of funds
c. Exempt mental illness from its list of eligible disabilities
d. Provide nonmedical services for reimbursement as well

42. Which of the following statements about stress is INCORRECT?

a. Substance abuse is often increased during times of stress
b. Biofeedback provides immediate insight into physical effects of stress
c. Too much stress can cause the body to become distressed
d. All stress is harmful to the body

43. The Individuals with Disabilities Education Act (IDEA) requires public schools to:

a. Provide vocational training for students with disabilities
b. Provide educational programs to the entire school about different disabilities
c. Create an Individualized Educational Program (IEP) for every student in their special education program
d. Place students with disabilities in mainstream classrooms

44. Members of which ethnic background have the lowest rates of seeking treatment for mental illness?

a. Caucasian
b. Hispanic
c. African American
d. Asian

45. African Americans are more likely than Caucasians to have:

a. Bipolar disorder
b. Schizophrenia
c. Major depression
d. Social anxiety disorder

46. Susto, or a fright condition, is most commonly seen in people of which ethnicity?

a. Hispanics
b. Asians
c. African Americans
d. Caribbean

47. You are about to perform an initial assessment on a young woman who does not speak English well. How should the PsyR professional handle the assessment?

a. Gather the information from her chart to fill out the initial paperwork
b. Use a family member to translate
c. Contact your facility management to locate a translator
d. Speak slowly and use nonverbal methods of communication to get the required information

48. Which of the following is true about the Minnesota Multiphasic Personality Inventory-2 (MMPI-2) and cultural bias?

a. There is no bias present in the exam
b. Research has shown that Caucasians tend to show more symptom misrepresentation than other cultures
c. Research has shown that Caucasians tend to show more symptom misrepresentation than African Americans
d. Research has shown that African Americans tend to show more symptom misrepresentation than Caucasians

49. While admitting a Haitian woman to a psych rehab program, she mentions that she wants to visit with her spiritual healer as part of her treatment plan. How should the PsyR professional respond?

a. Using an empathetic tone, explain that this would not be allowed and she must follow the treatment plan set forth by the team
b. Remind her that it is only a 30-day program and that she can consult with her spiritual healer once she is discharged from the facility
c. Consult the rest of the team involved in her care to make arrangements for the spiritual healer to visit
d. Inform her that she can have visitors whenever she wants and that the facility would not need to be involved in her treatment with the spiritual healer

50. Which of the following statements about performing a cultural assessment is INCORRECT?

a. Performing a cultural assessment is not necessary; the client will tell you what you need to know as treatment goes on
b. Language preference, religious beliefs and traditions, family history and support system, degree of acculturation, and education level should be included in the assessment
c. A qualified translator/translation service should be present at all times when speaking with someone who does not speak English
d. The PsyR professional should ensure that the assessment tools and interview questions are culturally sensitive

Answer Key and Explanations

1. B: A quality psych rehab program should focus on the specific needs of each client. While the diagnosis is important, each client should have their program tailored to their needs and abilities. The individual should be encouraged to participate in the formation of their goals and treatment plan, and the staff should show confidence in every participant of the program. The ultimate focus should be on optimal normalization and functioning within society.

2. D: The ultimate goal of a psych rehab center is for its clients to set and achieve reasonable goals to work towards becoming a productive member of society. Less focus should be placed on the treating or curing of mental illness, but on the individual needs and abilities of each of the participants.

3. A: A positive symptom of a condition is one that adds to the experience of normal behavior. A negative symptom is one that takes away from normal functioning. Avolition, or lack of motivation, and anhedonia, or loss of will to do anything enjoyable, are both negative symptoms of schizophrenia. Delusions are the most common symptom of schizophrenia. Having a flat affect, or lack of emotional response, is also a negative symptom.

4. C: There are three stages of schizophrenia. The first, also known as the primary or prodromal stage, occurs when the symptoms first begin to appear. The second, or acute stage, is by far the most severe and debilitating. The third or residual stage occurs as the symptoms start to lessen, though they are still present. An individual may transition from one stage to another (and back) over the course of their lifetime.

5. A: A dual diagnosis refers to client having both a mental illness and a secondary condition, most commonly a developmental disability or a substance abuse problem. Both conditions must be addressed during treatment, not just the primary or dominant condition.

6. D: An objective burden is one that is easily identified. Subjective burdens are those that are less easily identified and are related to the emotional and mental strain related to caring for a mentally ill family member. All of the answer choices listed are objective strains, except for choice D, which is a subjective burden.

7. B: First-tier family members are the people who are most responsible for the day-to-day activities related to the care of the person with mental illness. They usually live with them and help manage their schedule and treatment plan. Second-tier family members are less involved in the day-to-day care, but are still involved to some degree. Periods of relapse are felt more acutely and sharply by second-tier family members.

8. B: The psych rehab practitioner and the client must work closely to develop goals that are both realistic and appropriate for the client. The client's family should be involved when the goals impact the family dynamic and family caregivers.

9. B: The first stage occurs when the family members need to learn about the disease process; they may be in denial about what is occurring. The second phase occurs when the family accepts what is happening, and often accompanies feelings of sadness and grief about the situation. The third phase occurs as the family members learn how to manage and deal with the mentally ill person's disease. The final phase occurs as the family recognizes the problems inherent in the mental health system, which often causes many families to become involved in advocating for the mentally ill.

10. A: Attending a survival skills workshop or a support group designed especially for the family members of people with mental illness can be a great resource. The family should also consult with the physician and other psych rehab program staff. It is not appropriate to speak with the client's roommate or other clients at the facility.

11. C: The GRACE method employs five strategies for improving communication and encouraging a client to reach his goals. 1) Create a Gap between what the client believes is happening and what his goals are. 2) Work with his Resistance by allowing the individual to observe both the positive and negative points. 3) Allow him to work at his own pace. 4) Show Confidence that the client will be able to achieve his goals. 5) Empathize with the individual to encourage trust and honesty

12. B: Albert Bandura was responsible for the Social Learning Theory, which theorizes that people learn about social norms and behavior by observing others. According to the Social Learning Theory, the following four elements must be present for learning to occur: paying attention to the world around them, remembering the acceptable behavior, motivation to change behavior, and the actual ability to physically copy observed behavior.

13. D: Biological treatment using medication is most effective for treating acute episodes or crisis situations. It is not used to cure the disease but rather to treat or reduce symptoms. Medications, including antipsychotics, antidepressants, and mood stabilizers, are most effective at reducing symptoms.

14. C: Traditional beliefs about recovery do not apply to psychiatric recovery because these conditions typically last a lifetime. Therefore, it is not realistic to expect that true recovery results in lifelong freedom from symptoms and a return to normal functioning. The rest of the statements are correct.

15. C: Skills maintenance is a very common problem (and not just for clients with mental illness). To encourage skill retention and application, clients must be given ample opportunity to practice the skill, preferably in a real-world environment instead of an instructional environment. PsyR professionals should continuously provide situations for clients to practice old and new skills to help them remain proficient, and not just rely on family members to assist in helping the client in practicing new skills.

16. B: Client-Centered Therapy requires a strong relationship between the client and therapist that is based on mutual respect and trust. It requires that clients be able to take the lead, using his therapist as a guide. The relationship must be open and honest, and focus on the belief that the client can make positive changes.

17. A: The work is covered by the Federal Rehabilitation Act. No more than 8 employees participate in each group, and a job coach is on site at all times to provide continuous support and training. Unfortunately, the participants do not have much choice in their job function; they are usually all assigned within the same unit or area of the company.

18. A: Employer education is a necessary part of supportive employment opportunities. It involves educating employers about the valuable contributions that people with mental illness can make. Employers are encouraged to not view hiring people with mental disabilities as being charitable. Current employer needs and concerns are assessed and managed.

19. D: Boarding homes are an excellent option for many people because of the low cost and intermediate environment between hospitalization and living at home. Residents at these facilities often complain of a lack of privacy, not too much privacy. There is great potential for abuse by poorly trained or dishonest directors.

20. C: Residential treatment facilities are able to monitor compliance with medication regimens, while boarding homes and lodges are not. In addition, residential facilities can provide additional support for activities of daily living. Lodges and boarding homes require clients to be more independent and be able to care for themselves.

21. C: The Fair Housing Act was passed in 1968 and is enforced by the US Department of Housing and Urban Development (HUD), not by a local housing agency. It prevents discrimination by landlords by prohibiting different renting or purchasing requirements for people with disabilities and also by prohibiting landlords from refusing to rent apartments to people with disabilities. Mental illness is recognized by the Fair Housing Act as a covered disability.

22. D: Under HIPAA, medical information cannot be shared with his or her employer, for marketing purposes, or with anyone the client did not request. Information can be shared with insurance companies, for the purposes of coordinating care with other providers or hospitals, and with governmental reporting agencies where the information could protect public health.

23. B: Medicare Part A covers hospitalization in a specialized psychiatric hospital for 190 days over the client's lifetime. It also covers hospitalization at a general hospital that accepts Medicare without a lifetime limit. Medicare Part B covers psychological visits to doctors, nurse practitioners, physician's assistants, and clinical psychologists who accept Medicare. Part B also covers diagnostic testing, group or individual therapy, and medication administration that must be performed by a practitioner.

24. A: While it is important for a client's family to be supportive of his rehabilitation, it is more important for the client to have insight into his own condition and recovery. The factors that should be taken into account include the degree of trust that the client has towards the PsyR staff, the interest and level of commitment that the client has in making positive changes, and whether the client has insight into his situation and what will be required of him.

25. B: A functional assessment is a tool that determines the skills that the client has and which ones he needs to work on. A resource assessment identifies the resources the client has available to him and which ones he would need for additional support.

26. C: The Life Skills Profile is an assessment tool only to be used for clients with schizophrenia. It is a 39-question assessment tool that close family members and friends of the client will fill out, and is used to gauge the client's ability to care for herself, her ability to communicate, and her ability to interact socially.

27. A: The Simulated Social Interaction Test uses 8 hypothetical situations that are stressful and used to test the client's response. The Assessment of Interpersonal Problem-Solving Skills uses videos of problems that have been acted-out to have the client describe the problem and potential solutions. The Social Performance Survey Schedule utilizes a five-point scale to measure the client's degree of comfort with certain situations. The Interpersonal Role-Playing Test uses a two-point scale to judge a client's role-played response on appropriateness and acceptability of behavior.

28. D: The etiology of a syndrome is also known as the cause of the disease. The most likely outcome is called the prognosis. Anything that is done to attempt a cure is called a treatment, and an action taken to lessen the effects of the symptoms on the activities of daily living is called rehabilitation.

29. B: The Life Skills Profile is a tool that is completed by the family members or a close friend of a schizophrenic client. The remainder of the assessments listed are to be completed by the PsyR professional.

30. A: Advance Directives are written directions for your preferences related to your care in the event you are not able to make your own decisions. This may or may not include who you want (or do not want) to visit, who will care for your children, or what procedures/therapies you would provide or refuse consent for. The use of advance directives in psychiatric treatment is relatively new, and the client should be advised to consult with their attorney or legal consultant.

31. C: The Brief Psychiatric Rating Scale is a tool used after a diagnostic interview has been performed and a diagnosis has been reached. The scale is used by clinicians to determine the severity of the client's psychiatric symptoms.

32. C: Side effects of psychotropic drugs include hormonal irregularities, changes in appetite, weight gain, difficulty walking, dry mouth, visual changes, seizures, low blood pressure, tardive dyskinesia (involuntary movements of the mouth and limbs), a shuffling gait, and muscular changes. Rapid heart rate is not a recognized symptom of psychotropic drugs.

33. B: Milieu therapy focuses on changes within the environment and how those changes affect the client. Note that environment does not refer only to the physical environment, but the social and cultural environment as well. Treatment programs should reflect this, and provide a supportive, orderly environment.

34. A: TCL case management, also known as assertive community treatment (ACT), or full support case management is most appropriate in this situation because it provides all of the support a client may need. The goal of this type of case management would be to prevent relapse and rehospitalization of the client.

35. D: Double Trouble groups were created to address the unique needs of clients with both substance abuse and psychiatric illness because NA and AA stress the avoidance of medication because of the potential for addiction. These Double Trouble groups help clients who need the structure of a support group but who also need psychotropic medications.

36. D: According to the Health Belief Model, a person will only change if there is sufficient motivation to change. The motivation could be fear of illness or danger, punishment, or loss. There must also be sufficient support and resources available for the person to make the change.

37. A: According to Bruce Tuckman, there are four stages to group development. The first is called forming, and occurs as group members maintain social niceties because they may feel uncomfortable starting a conflict. The second stage is called storming and occurs when group members begin to approach problems logically and honestly. Conflict may begin to arise within the group. The third is called norming and occurs as comfort grows within the group and between members. The fourth is called performing, when the point is reached where they are able to work productively.

38. B: Mental health courts aim to act as a liaison between the mental health system and the legal system, and are used to manage the unique needs of people with mental illness. Participation is completely voluntary. Though participants are held fully accountable for the recommendations put forth by the courts, less stringent sentences may apply. Referrals to mental health facilities, or to additional support services, may be provided in lieu of or in addition to punishment.

39. C: The prodromal phase of mental illness occurs when the client begins to have difficulty functioning right before the active phase of the disease. The acute phase is when the disease is most noticeable and the symptoms most problematic. The residual phase occurs during the time immediately after an acute phase.

40. D: SSDI is a taxpayer-funded program. To be eligible to receive benefits, SSDI requires that you have paid into the Social Security system to be eligible to receive benefits. A person can begin receiving benefits 5 months after becoming disabled. SSI, however, does not require that you have paid into Social Security to be eligible for benefits, and you are eligible for benefits immediately.

41. A: A 1915(b) waiver is a federal law that allows states to limit client choice of health care providers and medical services. It also allows states to use managed care programs to provide health care and use the savings from these programs to provide other services. Finally, it allows states to limit the providers who can work under the program.

42. D: All stress is not harmful to the body. In fact, small amounts of stress can actually be beneficial and the body has been designed to deal with small stress. However, too much stress can cause the body to become distressed and begin to show physical signs or symptoms. Substance abuse is frequently increased during times of stress.

43. C: IDEA requires that children with disabilities, mental illness included, have the right to a free education. Public schools must create IEPs for every student in their special education program. The development of these IEPs involves not only the school staff but the parents and sometimes the child. They must be revised every year.

44. D: Asians have the lowest rate of seeking treatment for mental illness. Asian culture tends to put great emphasis on acceptance and avoiding unpleasant issues. There can also be shame associated with acknowledging mental illness and a desire to take care of one's own family.

45. C: African Americans are more likely to have major depression and major phobias. They are also more likely to have physical effects of mental illness. Finally, research has shown that African Americans tend to metabolize psychotropic medication more slowly and may require an adjustment to their dosing.

46. A: Susto, also known as a fright condition, is seen most commonly in people of Hispanic background. This is thought to occur when the soul leaves the body, usually as the result of emotional or physical trauma. Symptoms include anxiety, sweating, anorexia, and gastrointestinal problems.

47. C: A translator should be used to ensure the accuracy and completeness of the requested information. A nonfamily member translator is ideal because sometimes sensitive or confidential information is needed; the client should not hold back pertinent details because she is embarrassed by the presence of a family member.

48. D: The MMPI-2 assesses for mental illness by looking for discrepancies in how the test-taker answers basic true/false questions. While the test can be very effective, it is frequently criticized for displaying distinct (and consistent) differences between minorities and Caucasians. The research has shown that African Americans tend to show more symptom misrepresentation than Caucasians.

49. C: The use of spiritual healers is very important in many cultures and her desire to use one should be respected. It is important, however, that the PsyR team coordinate with the healer so they can be made aware of supplements that the client is taking. Some supplements can interfere with certain psychotropic drugs.

50. A: Cultural assessments should be performed during the initial interview and throughout treatment. Cultural beliefs about medical treatment and mental illness can impact treatment and its success (or failure). An initial assessment should be performed so that the PsyR professional can provide culturally sensitive care from the beginning, which encourages the client to trust the staff. Language preference, religious beliefs and traditions, family history and support system, degree of acculturation, and education level should be included in the assessment, as well as the client's feelings about his disease.

How to Overcome Test Anxiety

Just the thought of taking a test is enough to make most people a little nervous. A test is an important event that can have a long-term impact on your future, so it's important to take it seriously and it's natural to feel anxious about performing well. But just because anxiety is normal, that doesn't mean that it's helpful in test taking, or that you should simply accept it as part of your life. Anxiety can have a variety of effects. These effects can be mild, like making you feel slightly nervous, or severe, like blocking your ability to focus or remember even a simple detail.

If you experience test anxiety—whether severe or mild—it's important to know how to beat it. To discover this, first you need to understand what causes test anxiety.

Causes of Test Anxiety

While we often think of anxiety as an uncontrollable emotional state, it can actually be caused by simple, practical things. One of the most common causes of test anxiety is that a person does not feel adequately prepared for their test. This feeling can be the result of many different issues such as poor study habits or lack of organization, but the most common culprit is time management. Starting to study too late, failing to organize your study time to cover all of the material, or being distracted while you study will mean that you're not well prepared for the test. This may lead to cramming the night before, which will cause you to be physically and mentally exhausted for the test. Poor time management also contributes to feelings of stress, fear, and hopelessness as you realize you are not well prepared but don't know what to do about it.

Other times, test anxiety is not related to your preparation for the test but comes from unresolved fear. This may be a past failure on a test, or poor performance on tests in general. It may come from comparing yourself to others who seem to be performing better or from the stress of living up to expectations. Anxiety may be driven by fears of the future—how failure on this test would affect your educational and career goals. These fears are often completely irrational, but they can still negatively impact your test performance.

Elements of Test Anxiety

As mentioned earlier, test anxiety is considered to be an emotional state, but it has physical and mental components as well. Sometimes you may not even realize that you are suffering from test anxiety until you notice the physical symptoms. These can include trembling hands, rapid heartbeat, sweating, nausea, and tense muscles. Extreme anxiety may lead to fainting or vomiting. Obviously, any of these symptoms can have a negative impact on testing. It is important to recognize them as soon as they begin to occur so that you can address the problem before it damages your performance.

The mental components of test anxiety include trouble focusing and inability to remember learned information. During a test, your mind is on high alert, which can help you recall information and stay focused for an extended period of time. However, anxiety interferes with your mind's natural processes, causing you to blank out, even on the questions you know well. The strain of testing during anxiety makes it difficult to stay focused, especially on a test that may take several hours. Extreme anxiety can take a huge mental toll, making it difficult not only to recall test information but even to understand the test questions or pull your thoughts together.

Effects of Test Anxiety

Test anxiety is like a disease—if left untreated, it will get progressively worse. Anxiety leads to poor performance, and this reinforces the feelings of fear and failure, which in turn lead to poor performances on subsequent tests. It can grow from a mild nervousness to a crippling condition. If allowed to progress, test anxiety can have a big impact on your schooling, and consequently on your future.

Test anxiety can spread to other parts of your life. Anxiety on tests can become anxiety in any stressful situation, and blanking on a test can turn into panicking in a job situation. But fortunately, you don't have to let anxiety rule your testing and determine your grades. There are a number of relatively simple steps you can take to move past anxiety and function normally on a test and in the rest of life.

Physical Steps for Beating Test Anxiety

While test anxiety is a serious problem, the good news is that it can be overcome. It doesn't have to control your ability to think and remember information. While it may take time, you can begin taking steps today to beat anxiety.

Just as your first hint that you may be struggling with anxiety comes from the physical symptoms, the first step to treating it is also physical. Rest is crucial for having a clear, strong mind. If you are tired, it is much easier to give in to anxiety. But if you establish good sleep habits, your body and mind will be ready to perform optimally, without the strain of exhaustion. Additionally, sleeping well helps you to retain information better, so you're more likely to recall the answers when you see the test questions.

Getting good sleep means more than going to bed on time. It's important to allow your brain time to relax. Take study breaks from time to time so it doesn't get overworked, and don't study right before bed. Take time to rest your mind before trying to rest your body, or you may find it difficult to fall asleep.

Along with sleep, other aspects of physical health are important in preparing for a test. Good nutrition is vital for good brain function. Sugary foods and drinks may give a burst of energy but this burst is followed by a crash, both physically and emotionally. Instead, fuel your body with protein and vitamin-rich foods.

Also, drink plenty of water. Dehydration can lead to headaches and exhaustion, especially if your brain is already under stress from the rigors of the test. Particularly if your test is a long one, drink water during the breaks. And if possible, take an energy-boosting snack to eat between sections.

Along with sleep and diet, a third important part of physical health is exercise. Maintaining a steady workout schedule is helpful, but even taking 5-minute study breaks to walk can help get your blood pumping faster and clear your head. Exercise also releases endorphins, which contribute to a positive feeling and can help combat test anxiety.

When you nurture your physical health, you are also contributing to your mental health. If your body is healthy, your mind is much more likely to be healthy as well. So take time to rest, nourish your body with healthy food and water, and get moving as much as possible. Taking these physical steps will make you stronger and more able to take the mental steps necessary to overcome test anxiety.

Mental Steps for Beating Test Anxiety

Working on the mental side of test anxiety can be more challenging, but as with the physical side, there are clear steps you can take to overcome it. As mentioned earlier, test anxiety often stems from lack of preparation, so the obvious solution is to prepare for the test. Effective studying may be the most important weapon you have for beating test anxiety, but you can and should employ several other mental tools to combat fear.

First, boost your confidence by reminding yourself of past success—tests or projects that you aced. If you're putting as much effort into preparing for this test as you did for those, there's no reason you should expect to fail here. Work hard to prepare; then trust your preparation.

Second, surround yourself with encouraging people. It can be helpful to find a study group, but be sure that the people you're around will encourage a positive attitude. If you spend time with others who are anxious or cynical, this will only contribute to your own anxiety. Look for others who are motivated to study hard from a desire to succeed, not from a fear of failure.

Third, reward yourself. A test is physically and mentally tiring, even without anxiety, and it can be helpful to have something to look forward to. Plan an activity following the test, regardless of the outcome, such as going to a movie or getting ice cream.

When you are taking the test, if you find yourself beginning to feel anxious, remind yourself that you know the material. Visualize successfully completing the test. Then take a few deep, relaxing breaths and return to it. Work through the questions carefully but with confidence, knowing that you are capable of succeeding.

Developing a healthy mental approach to test taking will also aid in other areas of life. Test anxiety affects more than just the actual test—it can be damaging to your mental health and even contribute to depression. It's important to beat test anxiety before it becomes a problem for more than testing.

Study Strategy

Being prepared for the test is necessary to combat anxiety, but what does being prepared look like? You may study for hours on end and still not feel prepared. What you need is a strategy for test prep. The next few pages outline our recommended steps to help you plan out and conquer the challenge of preparation.

Step 1: Scope Out the Test

Learn everything you can about the format (multiple choice, essay, etc.) and what will be on the test. Gather any study materials, course outlines, or sample exams that may be available. Not only will this help you to prepare, but knowing what to expect can help to alleviate test anxiety.

Step 2: Map Out the Material

Look through the textbook or study guide and make note of how many chapters or sections it has. Then divide these over the time you have. For example, if a book has 15 chapters and you have five days to study, you need to cover three chapters each day. Even better, if you have the time, leave an extra day at the end for overall review after you have gone through the material in depth.

If time is limited, you may need to prioritize the material. Look through it and make note of which sections you think you already have a good grasp on, and which need review. While you are studying, skim quickly through the familiar sections and take more time on the challenging parts. Write out your plan so you don't get lost as you go. Having a written plan also helps you feel more in control of the study, so anxiety is less likely to arise from feeling overwhelmed at the amount to cover.

Step 3: Gather Your Tools

Decide what study method works best for you. Do you prefer to highlight in the book as you study and then go back over the highlighted portions? Or do you type out notes of the important information? Or is it helpful to make flashcards that you can carry with you? Assemble the pens, index cards, highlighters, post-it notes, and any other materials you may need so you won't be distracted by getting up to find things while you study.

If you're having a hard time retaining the information or organizing your notes, experiment with different methods. For example, try color-coding by subject with colored pens, highlighters, or post-it notes. If you learn better by hearing, try recording yourself reading your notes so you can listen while in the car, working out, or simply sitting at your desk. Ask a friend to quiz you from your flashcards, or try teaching someone the material to solidify it in your mind.

Step 4: Create Your Environment

It's important to avoid distractions while you study. This includes both the obvious distractions like visitors and the subtle distractions like an uncomfortable chair (or a too-comfortable couch that makes you want to fall asleep). Set up the best study environment possible: good lighting and a comfortable work area. If background music helps you focus, you may want to turn it on, but otherwise keep the room quiet. If you are using a computer to take notes, be sure you don't have any other windows open, especially applications like social media, games, or anything else that could distract you. Silence your phone and turn off notifications. Be sure to keep water close by so you stay hydrated while you study (but avoid unhealthy drinks and snacks).

Also, take into account the best time of day to study. Are you freshest first thing in the morning? Try to set aside some time then to work through the material. Is your mind clearer in the afternoon or evening? Schedule your study session then. Another method is to study at the same time of day that you will take the test, so that your brain gets used to working on the material at that time and will be ready to focus at test time.

Step 5: Study!

Once you have done all the study preparation, it's time to settle into the actual studying. Sit down, take a few moments to settle your mind so you can focus, and begin to follow your study plan. Don't give in to distractions or let yourself procrastinate. This is your time to prepare so you'll be ready to fearlessly approach the test. Make the most of the time and stay focused.

Of course, you don't want to burn out. If you study too long you may find that you're not retaining the information very well. Take regular study breaks. For example, taking five minutes out of every hour to walk briskly, breathing deeply and swinging your arms, can help your mind stay fresh.

As you get to the end of each chapter or section, it's a good idea to do a quick review. Remind yourself of what you learned and work on any difficult parts. When you feel that you've mastered the material, move on to the next part. At the end of your study session, briefly skim through your notes again.

But while review is helpful, cramming last minute is NOT. If at all possible, work ahead so that you won't need to fit all your study into the last day. Cramming overloads your brain with more information than it can process and retain, and your tired mind may struggle to recall even previously learned information when it is overwhelmed with last-minute study. Also, the urgent nature of cramming and the stress placed on your brain contribute to anxiety. You'll be more likely to go to the test feeling unprepared and having trouble thinking clearly.

So don't cram, and don't stay up late before the test, even just to review your notes at a leisurely pace. Your brain needs rest more than it needs to go over the information again. In fact, plan to finish your studies by noon or early afternoon the day before the test. Give your brain the rest of the day to relax or focus on other things, and get a good night's sleep. Then you will be fresh for the test and better able to recall what you've studied.

Step 6: Take a Practice Test

Many courses offer sample tests, either online or in the study materials. This is an excellent resource to check whether you have mastered the material, as well as to prepare for the test format and environment.

Check the test format ahead of time: the number of questions, the type (multiple choice, free response, etc.), and the time limit. Then create a plan for working through them. For example, if you have 30 minutes to take a 60-question test, your limit is 30 seconds per question. Spend less time on the questions you know well so that you can take more time on the difficult ones.

If you have time to take several practice tests, take the first one open book, with no time limit. Work through the questions at your own pace and make sure you fully understand them. Gradually work up to taking a test under test conditions: sit at a desk with all study materials put away and set a timer. Pace yourself to make sure you finish the test with time to spare and go back to check your answers if you have time.

After each test, check your answers. On the questions you missed, be sure you understand why you missed them. Did you misread the question (tests can use tricky wording)? Did you forget the information? Or was it something you hadn't learned? Go back and study any shaky areas that the practice tests reveal.

Taking these tests not only helps with your grade, but also aids in combating test anxiety. If you're already used to the test conditions, you're less likely to worry about it, and working through tests until you're scoring well gives you a confidence boost. Go through the practice tests until you feel comfortable, and then you can go into the test knowing that you're ready for it.

Test Tips

On test day, you should be confident, knowing that you've prepared well and are ready to answer the questions. But aside from preparation, there are several test day strategies you can employ to maximize your performance.

First, as stated before, get a good night's sleep the night before the test (and for several nights before that, if possible). Go into the test with a fresh, alert mind rather than staying up late to study.

Try not to change too much about your normal routine on the day of the test. It's important to eat a nutritious breakfast, but if you normally don't eat breakfast at all, consider eating just a protein bar. If you're a coffee drinker, go ahead and have your normal coffee. Just make sure you time it so that the caffeine doesn't wear off right in the middle of your test. Avoid sugary beverages, and drink enough water to stay hydrated but not so much that you need a restroom break 10 minutes into the test. If your test isn't first thing in the morning, consider going for a walk or doing a light workout before the test to get your blood flowing.

Allow yourself enough time to get ready, and leave for the test with plenty of time to spare so you won't have the anxiety of scrambling to arrive in time. Another reason to be early is to select a good seat. It's helpful to sit away from doors and windows, which can be distracting. Find a good seat, get out your supplies, and settle your mind before the test begins.

When the test begins, start by going over the instructions carefully, even if you already know what to expect. Make sure you avoid any careless mistakes by following the directions.

Then begin working through the questions, pacing yourself as you've practiced. If you're not sure on an answer, don't spend too much time on it, and don't let it shake your confidence. Either skip it and come back later, or eliminate as many wrong answers as possible and guess among the remaining ones. Don't dwell on these questions as you continue—put them out of your mind and focus on what lies ahead.

Be sure to read all of the answer choices, even if you're sure the first one is the right answer. Sometimes you'll find a better one if you keep reading. But don't second-guess yourself if you do immediately know the answer. Your gut instinct is usually right. Don't let test anxiety rob you of the information you know.

If you have time at the end of the test (and if the test format allows), go back and review your answers. Be cautious about changing any, since your first instinct tends to be correct, but make sure you didn't misread any of the questions or accidentally mark the wrong answer choice. Look over any you skipped and make an educated guess.

At the end, leave the test feeling confident. You've done your best, so don't waste time worrying about your performance or wishing you could change anything. Instead, celebrate the successful completion of this test. And finally, use this test to learn how to deal with anxiety even better next time.

Review Video: Test Anxiety
Visit mometrix.com/academy and enter code: 100340

Important Qualification

Not all anxiety is created equal. If your test anxiety is causing major issues in your life beyond the classroom or testing center, or if you are experiencing troubling physical symptoms related to your anxiety, it may be a sign of a serious physiological or psychological condition. If this sounds like your situation, we strongly encourage you to seek professional help.

Online Resources

Due to our efforts to try to keep this book to a manageable length, we've created a link that will give you access to all of your online resources:

mometrix.com/resources719/cprp

It's Your Moment, Let's Celebrate It!

Share your story @mometrixtestpreparation